CHILDREN
of the
REVOLUTION

Books by Jonathan Kozol

DEATH AT AN EARLY AGE

FREE SCHOOLS

THE NIGHT IS DARK AND I AM FAR FROM HOME

CHILDREN OF THE REVOLUTION

Jonathan Kozol

CHILDREN of the REVOLUTION

A Yankee Teacher in the Cuban Schools

DELACORTE PRESS/NEW YORK

Published by
Delacorte Press
1 Dag Hammarskjold Plaza
New York, N.Y. 10017

Portions of this work originally appeared in *Saturday Review*.

Manufactured in the United States of America

First printing

Design and Typography by Giorgetta Bell McRee

LIBRARY OF CONGRESS CATALOGING IN PUBLICATION DATA

Kozol, Jonathan.
Children of the revolution.

Bibliography: p.
1. Education—Cuba—History. I. Title.
LA486.K69   370′.97291   78–18522

ISBN 0–440–00982–0

To Marisela, Mario, and Sandra,
three children of the Cuban revolution:
long hours, difficult days,
rewarding lives.

I never could have known that people lived in such conditions. I was the child of an educated, comfortable family. Those months, for me, were like the stories I have heard about conversion to a new religion. It was, for me, the dying of an old life and the start of something absolutely new . . .

I did not need to read of this in Marx, in Lenin, in Martí. I did not need to read of what I saw before my eyes. I cried each night. I wrote my mother and my father. I was only twelve years old. I was excited to be part of something which had never happened in our land before. I wanted so much that we would prove that we could keep the promise that Fidel had made before the world. I did not want it to be said that we would not stand up beside Fidel.

—ARMANDO VALDEZ,
former brigadista

CONTENTS

CONTENTS

PREFACE
by Paulo Freire

I cannot deny how difficult it is to limit this preface to the very few pages that were asked of me.

It happens that this book deals, in a clean and lucid manner, with a theme that touches me much as it did Kozol: the theme of the reinvention of Cuban society, that of the re-creation of a people who, seizing their history in their own hands—making it and, in it, remaking *themselves*—find themselves committed to one of the most serious and profound revolutions that we know. It is a revolution which from the beginning and without a fatuous idealism became the ultimate teacher in itself, giving first place to the indisputable role of education in the process of forming the New Woman and New Man.

"Why," asked Fidel in 1959, "apparently ignoring all traditional considerations of a military character, far from constructing fortresses, do we transform them into schools? Could it be that the revolution runs no risk? Could it be that our revolution has no enemies?

Could it be that no one plots against it? Could it be that we are not conscious of the struggle before us? . . . Why is it that the revolution can turn fortresses into schools? Because," answered Fidel, "since January 1, the triumph of the revolution, each school has become a fortress of the revolution."*

As, with total involvement, I pursued the original text of *Children of the Revolution,* I began to know again that which was already known: that is, the extraordinary effort of the revolutionary re-creation of a people, an effort that only the blind refuse to see.

"We have to forge the true teacher," said Fidel, referring to the teachers of the future during one of his speeches in 1966, "true teachers in the most honest sense of the word, teachers capable of teaching not only in the city, but also in the country, not only in the country, but also in the mountains, and not only in the mountains, but also in the most distant mountains of the country.

"Teachers," proceeded Fidel, "not only capable of teaching in Turquino Peak, but teachers willing to teach in whatever part of the world a fraternal nation needs them. This is the kind of teacher we want to form, we hope to form, and we believe to be forming."

With the seriousness of an intellectual searching to unveil the truth and not to hide it, Jonathan Kozol speaks to us about the Cuban revolution, about the people reborn in its process, and recounts the extraordinary effort of its literacy struggle. He speaks about that which he saw and heard throughout his wanderings in Cuba. He hands over to us, vividly, the dialogue he held with countless Cuban revolutionaries. He analyzes the education that he saw in operation—not an education of

---

*For this, and for all other items of quotation or of public record in this book, see NOTES, beginning on p. 233.

which he read, or about which he was told. It is an education which, like any other, wherever it may be, can never be a neutral task.

Children of the Revolution will not, of course, dissuade in the least those who consciously set out to falsify the truth. In the long run I do not believe that Jonathan has written his book for people of this kind. The book clearly is written for those who feel already a certain degree of commitment to the Cuban revolution —and for those others, too (no doubt, a larger number), who still remain somewhat uncertain at this time, but who are willing to approach a revolutionary subject both with open eyes and with unfrightened minds.

Geneva, 1977

AUTHOR'S INTRODUCTION

On September 3, 1976, I found myself on board Cubana's Friday evening flight from Mexico City Airport to Havana. Because I was late, the Mexican customs agents—in their haste to check my bags and get me on the plane—forgot to stamp my passport. The same thing happened on my return at Montreal. As a result, computers will confirm that I have never been to Cuba. This will be the story, then, of a remarkable journey which (according to the files of those who know these things for sure) did not officially take place.

In seeking out the story of "the Great Campaign" of 1961—a major event in Cuban history and one which has a visible impact on all aspects of the Cuban schools today—I drew at first primarily upon the words and memories of the leaders of that struggle. Soon, however, I was able to discover a number of adults who had been part of the youthful teaching force of 1961—as well as several people who had learned to read during the course of the campaign and since have followed up with adult education programs that have led on to a university degree. In few cases did the words of the participants conflict with those of government officials. The same may be said in reference to my subsequent studies in the Cuban schools today. The words of the children at times surprised me and in every case intrigued me; in no case, however, did the confidential conversation of the children appear to stand in conflict with the claims of teachers, guides, translators, or high-ranking representatives of government.

If it is the natural inclination of all government representatives to try to give a visitor the very best impression that they can, it is the journalist's job to try very hard to get around that best impression. At no point during my study of the Cuban schools today or of the Great Campaign did I succeed in getting around the words of Fidel's top appointees in the Ministry of Education. There are a number of possible explanations for this perplexing situation. One—out of a large number—is that the leaders of a popular and unprecedented struggle of this kind find that it is natural and uncomplex to speak the truth.

A brief note on the language gap that proved (at first much more than later) to require a translator. If I do not specify the contrary, the reader may assume that I *did* use translation in almost all interviews that were arranged for me in 1976. (This period includes most of my research on the Great Campaign.)

Martha Acosta began this labor with me in September 1976 and later gracefully yielded to my wish to try out my increasing fluency in Spanish. She is a remarkable person, who handled the most difficult situations with immense dexterity, whether the need was for a sudden moment's interruption in an otherwise smooth-flowing session in one language or the other, or else for an eight-hour marathon of simultaneous translation between myself and two of the most rapid-speaking members of the Ministry of Education.

Martha would interrupt, when necessary, to ask for a restatement and at times a careful definition of a pedagogic term that she had never heard before. It was clear that she considered absolute precision to take precedence over her pride or a possible reprimand.

As my Spanish improved I was sometimes able to monitor the precision of her choice of words and did so consciously in areas of special sensitivity where I feared that she might wish to function as a buffer to protect me from a painful comment (at my own expense) or potentially disturbing revelation of a harsh or otherwise unpleasant aspect of the Cuban schools. Only once in all those hundreds of hours that we worked together did I catch a moment's hesitation on her part. It was, characteristically, not in an area that even touched on politics or schools, but in a bit of give-and-take that touched upon my private life.

When I returned to Cuba in 1977, Martha requested permission to accompany me once more. This time I did not require so much help, since I visited chiefly in the English classes of the secondary schools and there encountered teachers and pupils who were competent in English. When, however, a student's search for the right English word proved fruitless, Martha kindly interrupted to provide the necessary link. As rapidly as possible she then withdrew in order to allow the dialogue between me and the young boys and girls to pick up where we had left off.

When I was alone out on the street, I met a great many English-speaking high school kids or older men and women. The latter had learned English prior to the revolution; the former in language classes of the public schools. When all else failed, I did what I could in my own brand of Spanish.

A few brief postscripts on this subject: When Martha and her husband Pedro Sánchez spent a few days with me, Peter and I got on together in our high school French. Peter would often question me about "your Boston Symphony," which he admired very much. He also liked to reminisce about old Humphrey Bogart films like *Casablanca,* which are shown quite often in Havana on TV. When Peter and I conversed in French, Martha would appear to grow annoyed.

"What are you saying about me?" she would ask, all at once the one who was left out. If we persisted, she would threaten not to help me when I went into the classrooms the next day.

In retrospect, I realize how very much I learned, and came unconsciously to feel, about the temper of the Cuban revolution from these two reflective and generous young people—both of whom have had almost all of their education since the year in which the present government first came to power. When I was forced to undertake some difficult interviews at a time (in 1977) of great personal unhappiness, Martha and Peter proved to be the most supportive friends a stranger in a foreign land could hope to know.

Each of my two visits to Cuba was a pilgrimage and an adventure. I would like to thank Dr. Benjamin Spock, Senator George McGovern, and Congressman Robert F. Drinan for helping me to wade through all the oceans of red tape, both in Washington and in Havana, in order to travel ninety miles from our shore. I would also like to thank my friends in Cuba, Jésus Arboleya, Armando Valdez, Abel Prieto, and Raúl Ferrer—as well as my colleagues here at home, Judith Arnold, Michael Meyer, Beverly Bickel, Libbie Shufro, Elissa Kleinman and my editor, Jeanne Bernkopf. For critical comradeship of the most painstaking kind, I feel a special debt of gratitude to Lori Potter.

Finally, I thank the Louis M. Rabinowitz Foundation. If it were not for financial help afforded me by this fund, my travel to Cuba would not have been possible.

Part One

Cuba 1961: The Great Campaign

(A Nation Learns To Read and Write)

New York, September, 1960

I first heard of the Cuban literacy struggle while teaching at the CIDOC center, outside Cuernavaca, Mexico, in 1969. At that time CIDOC was a bustling crossroads of ideas and people of all possible political positions: radical Catholics, conventional U.S. educators, Piaget scholars from Australia, Swiss and British Marxists, recent exiles from the Latin nations. . . .

It was in that setting that I first met Paulo Freire. Many of Friere's words and recollections—stories of his arrest and near-assassination in Brazil, his subsequent friendship with Salvador Allende, his interest in the struggles of poor people in the U.S.—began to have tremendous impact on my thinking. One subject stirred me more than any other. It was Freire's reference to the literacy work that had begun in Cuba just about eight years before.

Following our conversation, I poked around the library of CIDOC—and struck at length upon a document that I had never seen on any education shelf in the

United States. Its title: *Methods and Means Utilized in Cuba to Eliminate Illiteracy.* Its publisher: The Cuban National Commission for UNESCO. I remember sitting down that afternoon in Cuernavaca and reading the eighty-page book from beginning to end. I left the center four hours later, convinced that I had struck upon the untold education story of the century.

After further discussion with Freire, I resolved to make a careful study of the Cuban literacy struggle and of its repercussions in the present educational system of that nation. It was a plan that I was obliged to postpone seven years. When I began, therefore, my first task was to reach back fifteen years in time. To my surprise, moreover, I found that I was forced to focus first, not on Havana, but New York. . . .

On September 26, 1960, less than two years after coming to power, Fidel Castro stood before the General Assembly of the U.N. in New York to present his first significant address before an audience which (because of radio, press and TV) would reach at least five hundred million people in almost one half of the nations of the world.

In a brief passage of this speech Dr. Castro spoke approximately one hundred words that marked the start of one of the most extraordinary educational events of recent times.

"In the coming year," said Fidel, "our people intend to fight the great battle of illiteracy, with the ambitious goal of teaching every single inhabitant of the country to read and write in one year, and with that end in mind, organizations of teachers, students and workers, that is, the entire people, are [now] preparing themselves, for an intensive campaign . . . Cuba will be the first country of America which, after a few months, will be able to say it does not have one person who remains illiterate."

4

Newspapers do not record whether any of those world figures who were present—Nikita Khrushchev, of the U.S.S.R., for example, or Adlai Stevenson of the United States—responded to this portion of the speech or to the back-breaking challenge which in two brisk sentences Fidel had just established for his nation. What *is* well known is that back home in Cuba the words of Fidel—above all, the promise of complete success in less than one year—came as a great surprise.

It is the truth, however, as a number of organizers of the literacy struggle recollect today, that the promise of Fidel was in general accepted with both energy and zeal by a Cuban population which had already been led by him to consider education—along with land reform and health care—to be one of the three most serious struggles which the revolution had to undertake.

Whether they were forewarned or not, the challenge that faced the Cuban educators was of very great proportions. According to the latest census, that of 1953, 1,032,849 Cubans were illiterate out of a population of a bit more than 4,000,000 adults. One out of four adults in Cuba, most of them farmers in small, isolated mountain villages far from town or city, could not read or write. The total teaching force in the Cuban classrooms on the day Batista fled (December 31, 1958) was thirty-six thousand. These teachers, moreover, were in large part obligated to remain in their jobs as teachers of children in the public schools.

The initial question, then, was not one of "approach" or "method"—but of logistics and manpower. Cuban educators were convinced that traditional teacher-pupil ratios could not bring the reading skills of middle-aged and older *campesinos* up to a functional level in the course of only eight or nine months. The ideal ratio, they felt, was one-to-two—although they were prepared to settle for a ratio of one-to-four at most.

Where could Cuba find two hundred and fifty thousand teachers for approximately one million people, living in the least developed and most isolated sections of Las Villas, Oriente, and Pinar Del Río provinces, where the highest rates of mass illiteracy conspired with the highest and most rugged mountain ranges to compound the task?

The answer—then, as many times again during the years ahead—came from young people. Cuba is, in demographic terms, a youthful nation, with almost half its population younger than eighteen. Only by the active intervention of young men and women could the nation possibly achieve its goal.

A call went out for student volunteers.

The call was answered by one hundred thousand pupils, almost all between ten years of age and seventeen. Exact statistics compiled by the Literacy Commission at the end of 1961 indicate that of this number, forty percent were ten to fourteen years of age. Forty-seven percent were between fifteen and nineteen. Virtually all the rest were under thirty. (The youngest "teacher" listed, a child named Elan Menéndez, was eight years old. The oldest "student," by way of contrast, was a woman of 106 who had been born—and grown up—as a slave.)

The student volunteers would soon be reinforced by over one hundred and forty thousand men and women, achieving a total teaching force of a quarter-million people. In the face of these remarkable statistics one obvious question is quite often posed: Why would so many Cuban students answer an appeal for work which (as Fidel warned them in advance) would not be easy, but would call for infinite patience, and would offer only gradual and piecemeal satisfaction?

The anti-Castro critic can provide a glib response: "slave-labor . . . Who can argue with a gun?" A mindless booster of the Cuban revolution might propose the oppo-site answer: "This is the magic of a socialist revolution." The answer does unquestionably have to do with revolu-tion—but neither with magic, miracles, or guns.

As veterans of the literacy struggle reminisce today, it seems apparent that the basic—or, at least, initial—motivation had a lot to do with the desire of kids (most of them urban, many middle-class) to share in an adven-ture which appeared in certain graphic ways to carry on the work-and-struggle-in-the-mountains symbolized by Che Guevara and Fidel. A kind of "ethical exhilaration," modeled upon these heroes, seems to have been the overwhelming impetus, rather than a tough, consistent, well-developed Marxist dedication.

Cuba, in any event, had not emerged as anything like a Marxist state in autumn 1960, or even in the early months of 1961. Without question many of the leaders were already committed to a socialist ideal, but this ideal had not been publicized or widely thrust upon the public mind. To miss this point, and to perceive the driving impulse as the consequence of Marxist discipline and dogma is, in effect, not just to miss the motivation but —far more important—to ignore one of the main *re-sults*. The fact is that socialist or communist conviction was not the major force that prompted so many thou-sand kids to spend most of a year risking their lives, working like fanatics, living on little more than six hours' sleep in the same house and often the same room (their hammocks slung above the same dirt floor) as some of the poorest campesinos in the land. It was *not* the major cause. It *was*, however, one of the most sweeping consequences.

To miss the crucial time-gap here, and to forget that Cuba first began its literacy struggle prior to any con-sistent work of ideological consolidation of its population, and prior to the Bay of Pigs attack as well, is to miss the far more serious and interesting point that it was the campaign itself which turned a hundred thousand liberal, altruistic, and utopian kids into a rebel vanguard of committed or, at the very least, incipient socialists, even if many still were far too young to know the fullness of the meaning of this word—and surely too young even to attempt to read the writings of Karl Marx.

There were, unquestionably, at least two other factors that awakened so much willingness for voluntary work and sacrifice. One was the unusual charisma of Fidel. Since by 1961 the largest numbers, of people who had opposed the revolution had departed for Miami, those who remained tended, by self-selection, to become part of a loyal, patient, dedicated phalanx for a campaign like the one that Cuba now began to undertake. The statement that "we would not allow Fidel to be embarrassed in the eyes of the whole world" is made today by many men and women who were only ten or twelve years old during the year in which it all took place.

In addition to all else there was the unquestioned impact of a massive organizing effort led to some degree by Marxists who already formed a close-knit vanguard in the Education Ministry—a campaign carried out to mobilize the kids through "propaganda." The word is used quite openly in Cuba, not as a critical term, but unabashedly, in order to indicate an undisguised, one-sided effort to persuade large numbers of the people to do something which they might not choose to do if they were not exposed to powerful arguments that had some chance to counteract a lifetime (or parental heritage) of colonial and class-oriented values.

Posters were displayed all over Cuba:

YOUNG MEN AND WOMEN,
JOIN THE ARMY OF YOUNG LITERACY TEACHERS . . .

THE HOME OF A FAMILY OF PEASANTS
WHO CANNOT EITHER READ OR WRITE
IS WAITING FOR YOU NOW . . .
DON'T LET THEM DOWN!

Perhaps the ultimate in use of propaganda depends, for its appreciation, upon reiteration of the fact that Cuba still remained a capitalist society in 1961. Certain major U.S. corporations still had the right to manufacture, sell, and advertise consumer goods. One of the most important firms, inevitably, was Coca Cola. Whether by duress, subtle or direct, or else under an impulse of good will, Coca Cola ended up by advertising reading skills: "In the Year of Education," read the Coca Cola ads, citizens still need "the pause that refreshes." Use that pause, the advertising writer said, "to teach a family how to read and write."

It may be that this is the only meeting-point in recent history of capitalist and socialist exhortations conveyed in the same words, presented by the same text, published in the same newspapers, and posted on the same huge signs along the road.

For all these reasons, then, and others too that will develop in the later pages of this book, Cuba found itself with more than one hundred thousand student volunteers. After a training period at Varadero Beach, and after the exemption of those who seemed unable to withstand the rigors of the countryside (those, for example, who were subject to asthma and would suffer greatly in the presence of the allergenics that exist on almost every farm), the final number enrolled for service ended up at 95,777.

The image of these young people, prepared to head out into the mountains, far from home, to share their literacy skills with those who were their elders by as much as thirty-five or forty years, became an eloquent symbol—and a bold historic challenge—for the nation as a whole.

II
Varadero:
The Lantern
and the Book

The training camp at Varadero opened in mid-April with one thousand students. Two weeks later there were seven thousand five hundred boys and girls in preparation; a few weeks after that, twelve thousand.

Cuban secondary schools were closed on April 15, elementary schools in early May. (A special program, "the Attendance Plan," was later instituted by the government to provide activities for younger children and for older students who could not participate in the campaign.)

The student volunteers were organized into a militant brigade, divided into a network of micro-brigades, named in honor of a Cuban youth, Conrado Benítez, killed earlier that year, three weeks prior to his eighteenth birthday, while he was working in a pilot literacy program in the hills. The young man, a black teenager who had recognized in Fidel's revolution the first important chance for abolition of racism in the Caribbean, was seized by ex-supporters of Batista, tortured, suffocated by the gradual tightening of a rope around his neck, and later mutilated.

He was only one of many volunteers who had been— or would soon be—martyred by the roving bands of anti-Castro forces. Another young man, Manuel Ascunce Domenesch, viewed today as one of the greatest heroes of the Cuban revolution, had requested—with a persistence that begins to seem endemic in the Cuban youth—that he be sent to do his work in exactly the same region where Benítez had been killed. He was housed in the home of a poor man, Pedro Lantigua. When the counter-revolutionaries struck at Domenesch, they also seized Lantigua—and took both the young man and the older man away to die.

"When you look at these photographs, when you look at Manuel's body," said the sixty-eight-year-old curator of Havana's Literacy Museum, a veteran soldier named Juan de la Cruz, "you may understand some of the feelings that we have about the CIA. Manuel first was given fourteen wounds by knives and bayonets. Then he was brought out to a tall tree with Lantigua. It is a tree from which the teacher and the farmer were hanged side by side. . . ."

The preparation given to each unit of the youth brigades was concentrated and extremely brief: seven to ten days at Varadero—an elegant former tourist spot about one hour from Havana, reserved in earlier times for foreign visitors, corporation representatives, and their Cuban friends, forbidden to blacks, whether North American or Cuban. With perfect symbolism Varadero now became the training site for those who soon would follow in the footsteps of their black co-worker.

Students were given instruction in the use of two essential teaching aids: a book of "oral readings" which would also function as a teacher's manual (*Alfabeticemos*) and the learner's primer (*Venceremos*).

Both are papercover booklets that the government prepared, after extensive research, under the direction of a well known Cuban scholar, Dr. Raúl Gutiérrez. (The press-run of the primer was one million five hundred thousand copies.)

In preparation of the primer, an exhaustive search was made for "active" words—words that bore associations of emotion, love or longing, ecstasy or rage among the campesinos. Using these words as starting points, the technical experts wrote the primer in the form of fifteen lessons, each lesson somewhat more difficult than the one before but each one reiterating basic sounds and themes. Each of the fifteen lessons was presented as a story or discussion of one of the "active" topics. Each was preceded by a photograph of Cuban life which served both to provoke discussion and to clarify the main theme of the chapter: an agricultural collective with three farmers briefly resting from their work; children and teenagers planting a sapling in the midst of an unforested terrain; Cuban fishermen holding up the catch from a day's work for "the cooperative"; a man walking out of the doorway of "the People's Store," his arms loaded with heavy bags of food and other goods; a couple standing in the doorway of their own small but attractive house; a mother receiving a child-care lesson from the doctor in a neighborhood prenatal class; a composite photo of a rifle, farmer's shovel, and the cheerful cover of the primer—symbolizing victory on all three fronts . . .

In a brief guidebook, *Orientations for the Brigadista*, students were instructed prior to the lesson itself to use the photographs to initiate informal conversation. "Avoid giving orders!" the young teacher was advised. "Say to the pupil: 'We are going to work. We are going to study . . .' Avoid the authoritarian tone. Never forget

13

that the work of learning how to read and write is realized and achieved in common . . ."

Another point, repeatedly emphasized within these guidelines, was stated in explicit terms during a conversation that I held with Raúl Ferrer, probably the single most inventive and most powerful figure in the literacy campaign, officially its vice-coordinator—and leader of the team that supervised the final preparation of the manual and the primer.

"The goal for us was to instruct the brigadistas not to try to imitate the condescending manner of the kinds of teachers they had known in public schools before the revolution. This was one-half the job of preparation.

"On the other hand, we did not want a random atmosphere to be the substitute for old-time methods of control. We did not want the aimless atmosphere identified with certain fashions such as Summerhill. We were dealing with poor people, and with people who were not small children but hard-working men and women, thirty, forty, fifty years of age. Then, too, our time was short. We felt that we could not await forever that 'spontaneous moment' so often elevated to romantic adulation in the literature that we receive from the United States.

"So we were forced to find a new path of our own: firm and clear, but not authoritarian; purposeful, sequential, and well-organized for pace, but never abusive, never condescending . . . We emphasized to the brigadistas that the campesino, even though he is an adult, is extremely vulnerable in many ways. Courtesy—not falsified flattery, but feelings of respect and of affectionate collaboration—seemed essential to convey right from the start."

In keeping with his cautionary words regarding "aimlessness" Ferrer defined a sequence to be followed in all lessons: "First, reading. Only after that would we ask anyone to write. The goal was to identify each written symbol with the sound it represents. By repetition, and in concord with the teacher, the pupil would master the specific sounds. Then we would ask each pupil to attempt a reading on his own. Once this was done, we would begin the breakdown and analysis of syllables ...

"If we did not enforce this much consistent and sequential work, one brigadista could not fill in for another in the case of sudden illness or the like. We also needed to keep track of every learner's progress and attendance: date of the first lesson, date of the last lesson, days when lessons don't take place—and why."

The orientation booklet carefully addressed itself to each one of these points:

First Step: CONVERSATION

Conversation between the brigadista and the pupil in regard to the photograph in the primer ...

(a) To find out what the pupil knows about the subject of the photo.

(b) To provoke oral expression.

(c) To clarify the concepts.

Second Step: THE READING

A complete reading of the text (block letters) that appears beside the photo:

(a) First, by the teacher: slow and clear.

(b) Second, by the teacher and the pupil at the same time.

(c) Third, by the pupil all alone ...

Third Step: PRACTICE AND EXERCISE

(a) Recognition of a phrase or sentence that has been selected ...

(b) Breakup of that phrase or sentence into syllables.

(c) Examination of each syllable within an exercise.

Brigadistas were instructed to keep diaries of their reactions, fears, uncertainties, and—particularly—errors (even *possible* errors) in the course of work in order to share this information with each other.

Interesting, as an example of undisguised political bias in the Cuban method of instruction, is the first active word offered to the peasants. That word, which is also the first chapter-title in the primer, is an explosive three-letter combination, "OEA"—Spanish-language version of the OAS, Organization of American States. By 1961 Cuba had begun to suffer economic isolation as a consequence of actions taken by the OEA after concerted pressure by the U.S. State Department. Farmers who could not obtain replacement parts for tractors or for other farm equipment would not ordinarily have a numb reaction to a term like "OEA."

One Cuban educator, Abel Prieto, said to me as I looked through the primer the first time: "It is the only time in history the OEA has ever contributed something of effectiveness to help the poor. They gave us their initials for the primer!"

The second active word and chapter title also in the primer is the acronymic "INRA"—the initials of a revolutionary organization, the National Institute of Agrarian Reform, that had just begun the labor of land-distribution to the poor.

Subsequent chapters of the primer, each preceded by a photo, deal with additional generative themes: "The Cooperatives of The Agrarian Reform," "The Land," "The Cuban Fishermen," "The People's Store."

The chapter on "The Land" starts out with three sentences in large print, each one standing as a paragraph of its own:

The campesinos now at last are owners of the land.

The campesinos cultivate their land.

The Cuban land is rich.

By the sixth lesson ("The People's Store") sentences are longer and the syntax more complex:

The campesino buys his needs both good and cheap within the people's store.

In the people's store there are all kinds of things.

The people's store is a cooperative too.

We now have more than two thousand people's stores.

Subsequent chapters grow at once increasingly difficult and also more explicitly political. Chapter Thirteen informs the campesino:

CUBA IS NOT ALONE.

It further states:

United we shall overcome aggression. They [i.e., the United States] will not be able to stop the revolution.

The same topics, words, and syllables and a number of comparable photographs and tales are also included in the teacher's manual, *Alfabeticemos*. Chapter headings in *Alfabeticemos* reiterate the generative themes: "The Land Is Ours," "The Right to a Home," "Cuba Had Riches [but] Was Poor," "Workers and Farmers," "War and Peace," "The Abolition of Illiteracy," "The Revolution Converts Barracks into Schools."

Both these books are intricately paced to build from single words to basic phrases, then to sentences and simple paragraphs, all of them resting upon the recognition of initial active words and generative themes, up to the point where writing and reading in themselves become the end result, whether the starting themes remain predominant within the learner's mind or not. It is difficult to believe, however, in the face of the coordination of so much verbal learning with so many powerful political ideas, that many campesinos would be likely later on to separate the knowledge of these words from their political associations.

Many of the examples offered in the passages above may well suggest to readers an approach to literacy that is identified with Paulo Freire. The Cubans, much like Freire's colleagues in Northeast Brazil, not only based their campaign on the search for charged and active (Freire calls them "generative") words but also insisted upon a dialogical relationship between the teacher and "the one who chooses to be taught." Even the prior exploitation of a photograph or illustration suggests the simple drawings used by Freire's colleagues to initiate the learning-process in Brazil.

To the degree that Cuban methods vary in some key respects from those used in Brazil, the differences can best be understood by recognition of the difference in the situations of the two societies. Freire's estimate of forty days of study, for example, to achieve a basic literacy skill becomes almost two hundred days in Cuba.

Of many possible reasons for the longer period of time required by the Cuban educators, the one most obvious explanation is that Freire's teachers were adults themselves—not young men and women barely out of grammar school or junior high.

Again, the more explicitly political nature of the reading matter used in Cuba, and the somewhat more directive role assumed by Cuban teachers (in their prior selection, for example, of a set of active words, rather than in the slow discovery of such words, as in Brazil), has to be explained at least in part by the embattled posture of the Cuban nation at precisely the same moment that the literacy program was begun.

It might perhaps have been left up to chance to see how many campesinos struck upon the powerful sound of "INRA" as an active word. It could not possibly be left to chance, however, to discover if the campesinos would be quick to strike upon a word like "OEA." It was regarded as essential to the national defense that isolated campesinos rapidly come to share a recognition of those formidable enemies that Cuba had to face.

Thus, although the campesinos in Brazil sooner or later came up with political words and phrases wholly on their own, many of which ("land," "owner," "doctor," "slum," and "hunger") were the very same as those that dominate the Cuban literacy texts, Cuba's educators were determined to assume a conscious role in helping to decide *which* of such words, and which of such phrases too, the campesinos would be likely to learn *first*. In a state of revolution, as Freire himself has said, certain things cannot be left to chance.

For all these apparent differences in both logistics and approach, the similarities between the Cuban struggle and the work of Paulo Friere cannot possibly be ignored. The similarity is no coincidence: Freire and Ferrer are warm and trusted friends. Their views have not been

borrowed, each from each; rather, they have been in-
spired by a common viewpoint and a shared experience.
Unlike almost all other educators of renown or power in
the present day, Freire and Ferrer have forged their
pedagogic views among the people that they have been
asked to teach, living in the villages and homes of the
poor people, close to the soil, toiling to win—beside
those campesinos—land and liberation both.

The brigadistas had to learn much more, however,
than the way to use the primer. They also had to be
prepared for life in the distant, largely unelectrified and
unfamiliar rural areas to which they would be sent to
teach and live. They had to be prepared to share in every
aspect of the daily work—whether it was that of farmers in the fields or that of mothers in their one-room
homes. The sense of solidarity that grew out of these
periods of shared labor seems frequently to have become the key to motivation, trust, and perseverance for
the teacher and the learner both.

Each brigadista was given a number of copies of the
primer and the manual, two pairs of socks, two pairs of
pants, two shirts, a pair of boots, a blanket and beret,
as well as a sophisticated multi-purpose version of the
Coleman lantern. Hammocks also were provided to the
brigadistas. (This was to avoid embarrassing the campesino families, few of whom would have an extra bed.)

The lantern was essential, not just to provide a light
by which to travel on the country roads from house to
house, but also to provide the light by which to carry on
the reading lessons in the hours before sunrise or during the evening when the farmers and their families had
assembled at the kitchen table.

Medical services were set up to assist the literacy
program in three ways:

(1) Physicians, nurses, and assistants were mobilized

to care for brigadistas in the farthest mountain reaches and most isolated villages of Cuba. This was essential to lessen the realistic worries of the parents and also to alleviate the many physical problems which the brigadistas, unaccustomed to the rural life, would very likely undergo.

(2) Doctors would also be needed to conduct a screening operation in search of those in the non-literate population who might have need for glasses. (When the screening process was complete, 177,000 pairs of glasses were distributed and fitted without cost.)

(3) Doctors and other health professionals were mobilized en masse to guarantee an almost puritanical supervision of the boys and girls while still at Varadero.

By May 15, when the training camp was operating at full strength, there were nine separate dining rooms, three hundred cooks, a hospital equipped to care for one hundred fifty patients at a time—and seventy-five large houses, old estates, and elegant hotels ready to accommodate a maximum of twelve thousand pupils at one time. More than one hundred expert reading teachers were also present to give the brigadistas their sole formal preparation.

To supplement the rapid-fire training given in ten days or less at Varadero, there were later to be regional sessions, generally held on Sunday mornings, at which an adult teacher met with a small group of brigadistas to help them plan their lessons for the week ahead. Of the thirty-six thousand classroom teachers, thirty-five thousand volunteered to work in this advisory capacity from the start of the campaign to its conclusion in December.

I asked on several occasions why there had been so much emphasis, during the sessions held at Varadero and in the Sunday morning briefings through the summer and the fall, on the issue of "the city to the country." Again and again the point was made that Cuba had been weakened for centuries by the isolation of the peasants and the consequent inability of urban students to identify with rural poverty and exploitation. One of the explicit objects of the literacy struggle was to build a sense of solidarity between these two important segments of the Cuban population.

One of Cuba's oldest Marxist educators, Dr. Mier Febles, would later summarize his feelings on the subject in these words: "The goal of the campaign was always greater than to teach poor people how to read. The dream was to enable those two portions of the population who had been most instrumental in the process of the revolution from the first to find a common bond, a common spirit, and a common goal. The peasants discovered the word. The students discovered the poor. Together, they all discovered their own *patria.*"

One former brigadista, Armando Valdez, now a member of the Cuban foreign service, summarized his own reactions in the course of conversation in September 1976: "I never could have known that people lived in such conditions. I was the child of an educated, comfortable family. Those months, for me, were like the stories I have heard about conversion to a new religion. It was, for me, the dying of an old life and the start of something absolutely new. I cried, although I had been taught men must not cry, when I first saw the desperation of those people—people who had so little . . . *No, they did not have 'so little,' they had nothing!* It was something which at first I could not quite believe.

"I did not need to read of this in Marx, in Lenin, in Martí. I did not need to read of what I saw before my eyes. I cried each night. I wrote my mother and my father. I was only twelve years old. I was excited to be part of something which had never happened in our land before. I wanted so much that we would prove that we could keep the promise that Fidel had made before the world. I did not want it to be said that we would not stand up beside Fidel."

Fidel himself played an important part in helping to create the atmosphere at Varadero. He was acutely aware of the kinds of intimate domestic situations in which the brigadistas soon would be immersed and wanted them to be prepared to understand and to respect the social mores and conventional sexual values of the rural areas in which they were about to spend six to nine months of work and life.

Juan de la Cruz, curator of the Literacy Museum, delights in telling a short story to illustrate the "moral rectitude" of supervision at the Varadero camp.

"One night," he said to me, "Fidel came to the camp. He was just like that—coming without warning. He wanted to see if everything there was moving along all right . . .

"He came, by accident, to the section which was set aside for girls. Of course, he didn't know! Nonetheless, it was a serious mistake. I was in charge of health and discipline, so I was responsible for carrying out his own instructions. No men were allowed within the women's camp at night. The militia were obliged to order Fidel not to enter that part of the camp.

"He laughed but felt embarrassed at his own mistake. Then he said the parents of the children would be pleased that we were vigilant on their behalf. He told me I was fulfilling his direct command. He apologized for making a mistake. Then he backed up in his jeep and drove away . . .

"It seems a little thing, but it is just the kind of thing that one does not forget. That is one example of the reason why so many people feel about him as I do. He is not arrogant. He is aware that he cannot do something which he has already told us would be incorrect."

Fidel's interest in the work at Varadero did not end
with the personal deportment of the brigadistas, though
he was determined that they set an ethical standard for
the people—and especially the young people—of the nation as a whole.

From the beginning he immersed himself in almost
every detail of the literacy planning. During March of
1961, for instance, only one month before the literacy
campaign began for real, the Education Minister, Armando Hart, was obliged to make a six-week tour of
Europe. Fidel considered the campaign to be of such
importance that he selected himself as "acting Minister
of Education" until the minister returned—fulfilling
this obligation not just by supervision of the overall
plans but also by participation in the composition of the
teacher's manual. (Some of the sentences in the final
version are his own, according to Ferrer. Others, which
he regarded as inept, were wholly cut or cut in part and
then painstakingly revised.)

His activism and participation, though eclectic, were
at no point amateurish. His interventions were not
whimsical but based upon long periods of reading and
reflection. Even during a period of danger which the
literacy program later underwent—a period in which
there seemed an excellent likelihood of national defeat
and international humiliation—his recommendations,
though extreme, were not frenetic and, though drastic
in the sacrifice they asked of fellow citizens, were never
unrealistic.

Fidel's main role, of course, was not in the composition of the primer or the manual, nor in the supervision
of the social atmosphere at Varadero. It was in his exhortation of the youth and his unstinting efforts to reduce the worries of their parents. This was especially
true of brigadistas who were only ten or twelve years
old: above all, those who had been assigned to sections

of the Escambray where anti-Castro groups remained a constant threat.

Fidel spoke many times at Varadero. There is a particular speech I have in mind, however, which seems to me one of the most sensitive and memorable of all. The speech suggests that Fidel is a great deal more than commonly concerned with the entire issue of respect for parents—and the loyalties between a parent and a child. Even the day of the address was carefully selected: Mother's Day, 1961.

"When you return to your homes," he said to the young people, "you will . . . be less demanding and more understanding of your parents. After you have learned to live . . . without television, without theaters . . . without paved streets . . . the chances are that you will never again find the soup at home tasteless—or the meat [too] tough. When you sit down again at the tables in your homes, even though they be modest tables (and, however modest they may be, the tables of the campesinos are more modest), you will feel grateful for the efforts and the sacrifices that your parents make. . . ."

On several occasions when it might seem that he was speaking to the brigadistas, it is self-evident that their parents were the audience he had foremost in mind. "The fact is that we are responsible to your parents . . . For them it is a sacrifice to be separated from you . . . We are very grateful for this sacrifice . . . It also places us under an obligation . . ."

In rereading this speech I am reminded of the words of Abel Prieto, former Minister of Elementary Education, who told me that Fidel had asked the Ministry of Education during 1976 to emphasize "courtesy" of every kind in classroom education. Prieto took it upon himself to write a little book, for classroom use, on courtesy to fellow human beings as "revolutionary style"—but, above all, courtesy to parents and the old . . .

Fidel's most passionate words at Varadero were, of course, saved for the brigadistas. It was they—and not their mothers or their fathers—who had volunteered to do the job, to risk their lives, in order to redeem the promise of Fidel before the world.

"You are going to teach," he said to several thousand brigadistas as they stood before him, "but as you teach you will also learn. You are going to learn much more than you can possibly teach and in the end you will feel as grateful to the campesinos as the campesinos will feel to you for teaching them to read and write. . . ."

The emphasis throughout his speech was on the intimate relationship, the mutual reliance, of the city and the country: "You will have the opportunity to see how the campesinos work in order to supply the cities and how each cup of coffee that we drink owes its existence to a thousand sacrifices by those campesinos. Year after year those campesinos . . . who have lived forever under the danger of eviction, have been creating wealth . . . You will come to recognize that every grain of coffee has its history of sacrifice and human efforts. Students receive books and scholarships . . . Where do these books and scholarships come from? Where does their food come from? Where do the clothes [of students] come from? That food, those books, and that clothing come from the people . . .

"The nation does not have these goods available because they fell out of the sky. The nation has these goods because they are the product of the labor of the people . . . Wealth is created by the manual worker, as well as by the intellectual . . . Part of the wealth is dedicated to you. Those same campesinos that you are going to teach are also working so that you can have your teachers and your good schools . . . Go from here

conscious of the fact that you are going to work for
those who, up to now, have worked for *you* ... Go from
here conscious that these people will return one hundred
fold what you are giving them. . . ."

He ended on an optimistic note: "You are the ones
who, starting tomorrow, will have to carry on this work.
That is why we are preoccupied with youth . . . We
believe that you will be better revolutionaries than we
. . . more disciplined, better trained, more free from
prejudice ... more competent in all ways to carry on this
work . . .

"I wish you success! I wish you victory! ... I hope that
you will bring back honor to our country. I hope that you
will win the hearts of the campesinos! I hope that you
will always feel a sense of pride for what you are now
setting forth to do!"

III

The Great Campaign

In the conversation today of those who were participants in the Great Campaign there remains a note of unforgettable nostalgia. Those others who, for various reasons, were not able to participate speak of this with deepest disappointment—almost a sense of shame.

The campaign clearly was much more than a pedagogic act. It was a moment of political and moral transformation for large numbers of young people who had never before been outside of the circle of their homes. As adults tell these stories to me now, it is also apparent that there was wide variation in the pedagogic challenges faced by various members of the youth brigades. Some devoted the entire period from May until December to uninterrupted work with just one family—often finding it essential to devote four-hour sessions to one person at a time. Others worked with a mother and grandmother in the morning, proceeded to the fields to help the father and son in their farm labor in the afternoon, returned again, after the sun went down—by lantern-light—to teach those men to write and read.

Others found that they were able to complete their work with two or three illiterates in one location in a period of only three or four months and then move on to spend another four or five months with another group of people in another town nearby.

Certain factors, however, seem to have been constant. The teacher-pupil ratio seldom passed the pre-established norm of one-to-two—or, at the highest, one-to-four. The primer and the manual were the universal textbooks of the program, as the lantern was its symbol and the challenge of Fidel its constant spur.

In looking back upon the sweep and the momentum of the Great Campaign, Dr. Ferrer recalls a conversation with Fidel before the work got underway. "We must do it," said Fidel, "with the whole people—and by an heroic rhythm."

It is that "rhythm" which remains so vivid as I listen to the stories both of those who were the front-line brigadistas and those who were the peasant learners. "I confess I am a fanatic on this subject," said Juan de la Cruz, speaking to me in 1976. "I could see the dedication of my people. I did not want to hold back from participation in an hour of history that had become my own. I felt it was my duty to attempt to teach my people how to read and write.

"So I worked first at Varadero, then in Oriente with the youth brigades—teaching, but also being held responsible for supervision of the youth and for detection of the weak spots in their work.

"Today, I am an old man, but I still have a responsibility to serve the goals and struggles of our state. I know that many dreams have been betrayed in recent times and many revolutions are not honest revolutions. They drive out one insane dictator to install another. It is my belief in this respect that Cuba has filled a role unique in recent times. We have made a revolution, but we have not allowed ourselves to be betrayed.

"Our revolution is an idealistic revolution. I do not mean to say it is utopian. Utopian revolutions are romantic, but they don't survive. Our revolution set out with a certain set of ethical ideals. We have adjusted some of our ideals to unanticipated needs, but we have never undermined the principles with which we first began.

"I have told you before, but I would like to say it to you once again because you may forget it easily in all the hours of talk that you have heard and all the notes that you have made. This—what I have told you—is the reason that I feel so much affection for Fidel. This is the reason that I cannot say enough of his good character, of his humility and hope. He makes me feel I still have an important role . . . even today . . . even at my age . . .

"In the United States, from what I understand, men of my age are put on welfare—then are given just enough to eat and sleep, as presents from the state. In our revolution I am not receiving presents from the state or my prime minister. I am working in essential labor. I am instructing many, many foreigners who come to visit us each year from far away. I am telling them the story of our Great Campaign.

"This is my contribution to the people—to the revolution. I hope that I can keep on in this work until it is my time to die."

There are many ways to tell the story of the Great Campaign. I would like to do it through the stories that were shared with me by one man and one woman, each of whom played a personal role in bringing about the victory of that campaign. Both were young. Both were bold, courageous, but untested. Both were members of the youth brigades.

Each told a story that was somehow special, yet each one spoke for many thousands more . . .

María was born in 1945 in Manzanillo, in what was then the largest and poorest province of the nation, Oriente. At the time that Fidel came to power she was a shy and reticent teenager. Two years later, by the time that the brigades were formed, she was sixteen, politically committed, and viewed herself as an adult, a revolutionary, and a woman.

"I first heard of the idea of the campaign in a speech that Fidel gave after he came back from the United Nations. I joined in one of the original brigades to go to Varadero. There were fifteen members in our group . . .

"I knew nothing about reading, but I learned to use the manual and the primer *Venceremos.* My first motive, to tell you the truth, was not to teach. It was to be part of a great struggle! It was my first chance to take a stand.

"Conrado Benítez was already dead. Manuel Ascunce Domenesch would die during the next fall, in November. We were assigned to neighborhoods where we were needed most. I was assigned not very far from my home town of Manzanillo. In that neighborhood there was a lot of work already done by campesino organizers. Each family had agreed that they would take in one of us.

"I had gone to Varadero in the early part of May. It was during the last week of the same month that I met my campesino family."

María is a tall, intense and striking woman. Her hair is black and long, and pulled back from her forehead. Her eyes are dark. Her hands are constantly in motion as she speaks.

I asked her if the literacy struggle was the first time that she had left home for more than a few days.

"Yes," she said. "It was the first time. I was very homesick for a while, but my campesino family treated me with lots of love. There was a mother, Ana, only twenty-one years old; a father, Nenno, who was thirty-five; a little baby, who was a year old. There were other brigadistas in the region, too. We met for two days at the start just so that we would remember one another and feel close. All of us remained good friends right through the year.

"It was the campesino families, though, that made the difference for us all. By the end, that family seemed to be my family. Ana was like a sister to me; Nenno seemed to me just like my father.

"It was a small house, a *bohío* [shack] to be precise, but it had two separate rooms. My hammock barely fit inside the outer room. The floor was dirt. The front door had been made out of two leaves, fitted together somehow with two sticks. I had to attach my hammock to a pole. They said that I should come and fix my hammock in their room, because it was too cold for me beside the door. In the morning Ana and I would wash down by the river. Then we would pick corn together. In the afternoon and evening I would teach both members of my family. I would also teach a man who lived next door.

"Sundays we had good times together. I did go sometimes to the training sessions with the teacher who had been assigned to our brigade, but most often I did not. I preferred to stay with my own family and their friends. The kids, the campesinos in the area, Ana, and I—we used to put on plays on Sunday afternoons. I was the singer!"

She began to laugh.

"Things were so busy, there was not much time to think about our mothers or our fathers. I don't mean just the time we spent on reading—though I worked on that quite hard. There were many other things as well. One job, for example, was to help arrange the transfer from the former money [i.e., Batista's currency] to the new money issued by the revolution. We had to be sure that all of the old cash was traded in and that it was handled in an honest way."

I asked María whether one additional person who depended on a family for food would be a serious economic burden—especially at a time when rationing was taking place, in the wake of the embargo and the early economic problems of the revolution.

"My campesino family received my ration card. They received an extra quota of necessities because I was their guest. The food was not delicious. I did not expect that it would be delicious. Nonetheless, there was sufficient food—and all the basic needs, as guaranteed to every man and woman by Fidel. Some of the food was really pleasant, too. It was a good surprise!"

I asked her to speak in detail of the literacy work. María said that she had had one pupil (a young man who was a nextdoor neighbor) who could learn extremely fast. He was already twenty-eight years old. Her campesino family, on the other hand, did not have such an easy time.

"They were both at the same level. They were close to totally illiterate. Ana, however, learned much quicker than her husband. The methods I used were those I had been taught at Varadero. My only recourse, since I knew so little about reading, was the primer. It did the job. We never would have known how to proceed if we did not have *Venceremos* as our guide."

I asked about the power of the words that were the pedagogic backbone of the primer. "OEA," as I suggested to María, could not possibly have been a household word to every campesino. Where, then, was the motivation to acquire comprehension of this term?

"The motivation," she replied, "was certainly not just floating in the skies. It was prompted, and awakened, by the conscious efforts of the brigadista. It was our obliga-

tion to explain the meanings of the words we chose.
First we used the photo. It was a photograph of lots of
people in black ties and such—at one of the official sessions of the OEA. Then we led our students into conversations about what was taking place. We would explain
the meaning of a term like OEA, not perhaps as U.S.
diplomats would like us to describe the OEA but in a
manner that I think you, or even your government
today, would very likely view to be correct and true. I
would say something like this:

" 'We are looking at a picture of a meeting where the
North and South American nations came together to
decide on certain plans. One of those plans was to attempt to end our revolution by denying to us the medi-
cines and tools and trucks and tractors we would need
to carry on the revolution.' The attack on Playa Girón
[the Bay of Pigs] helped us to teach that lesson a whole
lot.

"Other active words—like 'INRA'—came, of course,
much closer to the bone. INRA was the means by
which our families won their livelihood: their land.
We went much deeper into INRA, therefore, and also
into other words and phrases of this kind. There, it is
safe to say that we did not need to provoke or to be-
stir. The motivation was already waiting in the earth
and in the air . . ."

I asked her for particulars of her own life during the
time that she was in the home of her new family. I
asked, for example, if she could recall the emphasis at
Varadero, on such possible dangers as discourtesy or
condescension—and if she could recall the application of
such warnings later on.

After a moment's pause, in which she closed her eyes,
she said: "I think that I can give a simple, but not very
elegant example. It seems even a little foolish now, but
it is just the sort of action that can make a difference to

a family of poor people when they have a teenage teacher as their guest. It may amuse you: I had to learn to eat my food, *all* of my food, using just a spoon. I had never eaten everything with a spoon before. I had always used a fork and knife. My campesino family used their spoons for everything. Well! I couldn't win my family over to the revolution in one night—or with one spoon! It took a lot of little things—like eating the same food as they, and working with them in the fields."

She laughed at herself, but then she added, "At least there never was distrust and there was always lots of fun. All those things depended on the willingness of everyone to try to make it a success . . .

"The lantern," she said, without a question to prompt her, "was essential. The old lanterns gave off too much smoke. The light they gave was dirty, yellowish light. [The old lantern used in the countryside before the revolution was hardly more than a blackened can of kerosene with a small cord extending from a narrow neck. Neither the height nor the intensity of the flame could be adjusted.] The bright light of the new lantern helped to make the house more cheerful. It made us all more willing to sit down and work, even at the end of an exhausting day."

I asked her if the lantern was a rugged instrument or whether it was fragile, as certain kinds of Coleman lanterns are.

"It did require considerable care," she said. "For safety's sake we hung it from the beams. There is one thing you may not know. We were allowed to leave our lanterns with our campesino families, as a symbol of our friendship, when the work was done . . ."

I asked María about the problem of exhaustion. How much could one brigadista do within a single day?

"I don't know why, but I did not get weary. I tried to finish up the night-time class by nine P.M. because we all got up at six. When Ana got up in the morning, so did I. She said to me: 'Why don't you sleep a little more?' I answered her: 'I want to go with you wherever you must go. When you go to the river, I would like to go there, too.' So it was in that way that we began to build a sense of solidarity together. It was a beautiful time in my life. Sometimes Nenno was late, because he had to cross the river every day to go to work. Then, of course, he had to cross it once again in order to come home.

"Even from the start, as I have said, the reading lessons were more difficult for Nenno. He said to me, 'I am not intelligent. I will give you a prize if you can teach me how to read.' He would say again and again that he knew nothing. Sometimes, as you know, it is a case of ruined self-esteem. Other times there is an element of truth in statements of this kind. It *is* a fact that he knew almost nothing of a verbal nature.

"During the months in which we worked together, it was as if he had to wrestle with his inner self, in order to turn himself into another human being. He wasn't a hero—but he makes me think of Che. He learned to write! He learned to read! He passed all the exams! He wrote a letter to Fidel! Ana and he both wrote their letters, but it was *his* letter which has always made me cry.

"Well! Now, when I think back, I can remember that we cried a lot that year. People in the country do not seem to be as frightened of expressing their emotions as we often seem to be. We cried, it seems, at almost any celebration. We cried at birthdays and, of course, we cried when someone had to say goodbye. When I left, I have to say that it was very, very hard. Ana and Nenno cried—and so did I."

She paused, as if she had recaptured the whole moment once again and was about to cry once more—but then went on.

"The train ride that brought the brigadistas to our final celebration in Havana was extremely long. First we took the train to Manzanillo. I remember that I cried when I got on the train. Half an hour later nobody cried, but we had all begun to sing. We sang a lot and as the train went on from town to town they added on new cars.

"The train grew longer and longer as more and more brigadistas—with their hammocks and their books and knapsacks—climbed on board. Workers and campesinos came down to the station in each village as our train came in. They came to cheer us on, to sing—sometimes to bring us extra food. We were all talking to each other —what would we do next? Everyone had a story to tell. Before the end our train had thirty cars. Many of the campesinos came on board to join the celebration in Havana."

I asked Maria whether she had already read a great deal in Marx, Martí, or Lenin at that time. She said that she had not. "Even in 1961 few of us were socialists or Marxists. All we had done was to respond to the first call of the revolution. We had responded to the call in order to pay homage to the men and women who had given up their lives during the fight against Batista. We were revolutionaries— yes!—but we were just beginners."

I asked her what was special, then, in terms of her own growth, about the Great Campaign. It seemed to me that by her sixteenth year she had already been committed to respond to almost any struggle that the revolution might require.

"This is the truth," she said, "but it had all remained abstract. The Great Campaign gave me the concrete knowledge, for the first time, of the forms that exploitation could assume. It also taught me something that

I had already felt but never yet had tested with my life, with my own mind, and with my hands.

"Che was our model; he will always be our model. But because he is a man, it is conceivable to misconstrue his vision of the future as a future in which women like myself would have no role.

"The literacy struggle was the first time in my life, and I believe the first time in our history as well, that women were given an equal role with men in bringing about a monumental change. Today we speak of the New Woman and New Man. It is a phrase that first came into common use only in recent years, but it began to be a concrete truth in 1961. As you have seen, it is a concept that is not forgotten."

Miguel was born in 1947 in Santa Clara, capital of what was then Las Villas province.

In April 1961, when he was fourteen years of age, he told his mother and father that he had decided to become a brigadista.

"I had to bring a paper home to get my folks to sign permission," he recalled. "My mother said she would not sign. I told her, then, that I would sign her name myself —or else that I would simply run away. My mother signed."

The group he joined was given only an abbreviated training session of three days at Varadero. Miguel was not certain of the reason why his training had to be condensed, but he told me he felt quite confident after those three days that he could do the job. "With the primer and the manual it was really not so hard. The hard thing was the distance—and the fear. We were going many miles from home. We traveled by train to Oriente. From the city of Bayamo we went on by truck. Some of us were sad at first, but there was a good feeling in the group. We sang some songs and tried to keep our spirits high. There were forty-five brigadistas in one truck!

"We were delivered by that truck to all the different neighborhoods in which we were assigned to teach. Our leader introduced me to the house where I was going to live. It was not a house, in fact, but only a small shack. It was so small that I could not hang my hammock in the single room. There was a mother, a father, and two little girls, all in that tiny space.

"My first idea was that we ought to build a bigger house before we settled down to read and write. The father thought it was a good idea. I was surprised. In fifteen days we built that house! It was a solid piece of work. That was my first attempt in the construction industry!"

Even today, at thirty, a father of two children now, he is still a small man: frail and thin. "We had to cut down trees, then cut the lumber. Instead of using nails we bound the corners of the wood with fibers. It was hard work, but I did not get sick. I never once got sick. In all of those ten months I never went to see a doctor.

"After all our work in building the house we settled down to learn. We would pick coffee beans in the morning and the afternoon. At night we would turn up the lantern and begin to read and write. At first I taught only one student—the father, since the woman did not want to start the lessons. In all honesty, she did not really want me to remain there.

"For fifteen days she would not speak my name. I didn't mind. I taught the man. I did the best I could. Then one day I noticed something that gave me a surprise. I saw that she was reading in secret when she did not think that I was there. I asked her: 'Please. Why don't you let me try?' After a month she started to write for the first time in her life."

The work, he said, was very hard, but he insisted that

the satisfaction far transcended every effort that he made: "We used to wake at five A.M. to work out in the fields. The mother was at home during the day to care for her two little girls. The old ways still remained. Then we would work more on the house and then at night we would sit down to learn to read and write. I struggled to teach the ideals of the revolution at the same time that I taught them how to read and write. When I left, that woman cried. Her husband cried as well. I also cried. They had passed their last exam and written letters to Fidel.

"All through the next two years they wrote to me. Their letters were beautiful, but they were very plain. They would ask me why I did not come back for a visit. I was in school, so I could not return. Besides, it would have been a long, long way. I always wanted to go back, however. I felt that I would have to go there someday when I was an older man. One day I *will* go back—not by myself, but with my wife and with my children, too."

I asked him whether he ever got a chance to rest during that year and also whether he received advice from older teachers when he faced a problem that he could not solve. He indicated that the supervising teacher was more of a moral backup than a pedagogic guide.

"Our teacher, who advised us, was a competent man. Moreover, he had worked with Conrado Benítez. That meant a great deal to us too. We felt he was our link to the great struggles of the past. He was twenty-three or twenty-four. He would explain things to us and would help us to resolve our problems. This was his job, but it was more the friendship that he gave to us . . .

"Whenever we met on Sundays, it was at a nearby river. We would swim and drink from little cans of Pet evaporated milk and pass around pieces of chocolate and tell jokes and read each other letters that we had received from home. Naturally, I missed my mother and my father a great deal. Communication was extremely poor. I received in all only three letters during the entire year.

"We used to play a kind of game to make it seem like we were all getting more letters. Anybody who received a letter from his family would read it out loud. We would each pretend it was our own. Maybe this will sound a little childish to you, but we were far from home. Even people who are almost fifteen years of age can sometimes feel like little kids . . .

"To be honest, Sunday was our day of celebration. It was the only day we ever had a chance to take it easy, to relax. We would go down to the river and meet and we would share ideas. We were not in danger, since we were in the Sierra Maestra. It was in the Escambray that most of the murders and intimidation were still taking place."

Just as Miguel's work came to an end with his first family he was shifted to another home—where the brigadista had gotten sick and had been sent back to Havana.

"The second family was much easier," he said. "The woman this time was the quickest. Her husband had a harder time, both in the reading and in writing. I began to teach the woman out of *Venceremos*. She needed many corrections in her spelling, in particular the use of accent marks, but, of course, the main thing was to teach the person how to read. In that respect she was prepared to help her husband a good deal. After a few months had passed, they both were able to complete the last exam. I also taught one of their boys—the oldest one of four. He knew already how to write and how to read, but he was eager to learn more. He was a mischievous and curious child. I taught him from newspapers and from magazines. You know, I never *did* forget that little boy . . ."

All of a sudden, as we spoke, his eyes lit up as if he had just struck upon a story, or a memory—or a joke.

"Not long ago," he said, "a few years back, I was with my family. We were walking in the park. Suddenly I saw a man that I knew I had met someplace before. He called: 'Miguel!' Then right away I knew it was that man!"

I asked him if he meant the father of the second family.

He told me "No! It was the first! It was the same man who had worked to build his house with me, right at the start! We talked a while and then he asked me how my life had been since he had seen me last. I said I was a student at the university now. He laughed and said he was a student, too! He was studying also—only he was following a course in agricultural technology. Then he would go back to his home village. It was a surprise for me, as you can guess . . .

"That year out in the country I had taught a little and I had worked a lot, but, as Fidel had promised in advance, I had learned much more than I could ever teach. The campaign did not depend upon Fidel. It depended on our faith in a new way of life. Of course, it is the truth that we could never find another leader like Fidel. He seemed to know the moment was just right for the campaign. He also knew the moment of Girón was just the time to start to speak to us about his socialist ideals. I did not know of Marx or Lenin at that time. I only knew about Fidel. I loved his courage and determination and I loved his openness, his honesty, and his imagination.

"I still feel very much the same way that I felt in 1961. It isn't just for what he has already done—but also for the things he dreams to do . . ."

IV
War
Footing

Those who are resolved to find the flaw in Cuba's efforts to eradicate illiteracy (on the supposition that there *has* to be one) often draw attention to the military language used by Cuban leaders to refer to the campaign. It is beyond question that a military fervor, openly avowed in the rhetoric of Fidel Castro, helped to fire up the passion of the literacy struggle from the start. There are, however, several realistic reasons for this military tone.

The invasion of the Bay of Pigs is only the most obvious. On April 17, at a time when student brigades had just begun their training sessions in the camp at Varadero, Cuban exile forces launched their ill-fated invasion of Matanzas province. Training in literacy instruction ceased for less than seventy-two hours while a number of leaders of the camp, as well as many older brigadistas, put on their military uniforms and headed for the coast.

The present Cuban minister of education commanded

the artillery at the Bay of Pigs while Fidel Castro led the tanks. Two days later, on April 19, the brigadistas were again immersed in preparation for their battle against ignorance and fear. "We were obliged to finish up one battle first—an easy one," said Juan de la Cruz. "Then we returned to dealing with the other battle, which, of course, was bound to be a good deal harder, as we all knew very well."

On the same day, and for two days preceding the invasion, Cuban exile forces launched a number of air attacks on civilian targets in the region of Havana, intended as diversionary actions. One such attack, whether by error or intent, took place on a public school. The air attack began during a sixth-grade class in social studies. Several pupils in the class had, only hours before, sketched out on a blackboard several words and illustrations that revealed their fears of U.S. intervention.

I have seen this blackboard, shredded at some points with the side-slash of bullets, pockmarked at others with direct hits. The blackboard was taken from the elementary school to the camp at Varadero and set up where brigadistas could not miss it as they went about their daily work.

These incidents, like the earlier murder of Benítez, led by inevitable logic to the military style and the military language of the youth brigades. The words "brigade," "detachment," and "campaign" came to be standard designations for the struggle now already underway.

Each brigadista was counted as a member of the *Ejército* (Army) of young teachers. Each was dressed in olive pants, a gray shirt, and an olive-green beret. A badge ("CB") appeared on both the shoulder and the chest.

In obvious ways the uniform helped to keep alive for each and every brigadista the dangers that they faced.

Counter-revolutionary forces still were operating in the Escambray and the Sierra Maestra (though somewhat less so in the latter region, since this was where Fidel and Che had been most active in their medical and pedagogic work during the period from 1956 to 1959 and therefore had won the strongest peasant backing.)

There was an additional reason for the military style. This was the whole idea of continuity with those who had been members of the revolutionary army from the start. Che and Fidel had dressed in just this uniform or one quite similar and each had sought to inculcate in the other the same sense of discipline and of self-abnegation for the three years from their landing on the coast of Oriente to the victory of the revolution at the start of 1959.

The prevalence of military terms, therefore, was a natural tendency: practical and symbolic at the same time. The words of Paulo Freire seem particularly appropriate: "Freedom is acquired by conquest, not by gift." The military flavor of the Great Campaign reflects this spirit every bit as much as Che Guevara's military struggles of three years before. The students were trained not to "approach" but to "attack and conquer" both illiteracy and fear among the poor. The mood was militant, not tentative: keyed to victory, not to "interesting results." The title of the primer was a declaration of determination: *Venceremos*—"We Shall Overcome." They did not say, "We hope to win"—"We rather think that, with sufficient funds, we might." Instead, they said: *"We shall."* In the event—though after desperate efforts and real dangers of defeat—they finally did.

In midsummer 1961 a sense of danger swept through the structure of the Great Campaign. The progress which the organizers had expected by this date was nowhere within reach. The whole timetable, all expectations of the solitary effectiveness even of ninety-five thousand highly motivated kids, seemed virtually to fall apart.

Organizers did not take long to respond to the alarm. Once they saw the figures for the first four months of the campaign, they set forth on a whole new phase of the attack—and, even beyond that, a step-up in the very *nature* of the attack—that represented something like a new start for the whole campaign.

The step-up was sparked, above all else, by the belated recognition of a single fact. While 500,000 Cuban adults were reported to be studying with the brigadistas by the final weeks of June, figures made public in late August showed that only 119,000 had been listed by their teachers as successfully completing the requirements of the course. With so little time remaining before the end of the campaign, the government set out to reinforce the brigadistas.

First, a call went out to factories with the hope of mobilizing 30,000 workers to create a new brigade ("*Patria o Muerte*") to augment the teaching staff within three days. The workers were promised their regular pay to teach non-readers in the mountains and the farms. Only 21,000 workers, according to UNESCO, answered the call: less than were needed, less than were requested, but 21,000 more than had been in the teaching force before.

Second, a coalition of mass organizations (Young Rebels, the Federation of Cuban Women, Committees for Defense of the Revolution) carried out, at government request, a massive effort to locate and to convince recalcitrant men and women not to be ashamed of their illiterate status but to join the learning force. The same organizations also formed ad hoc brigades of literacy workers. In this way the concept of the "People's Teachers" (neighbors teaching neighbors), first initiated during the early summer, came at last into full realization.

Third, the government ordered Municipal Education Councils (local school boards) straight across the nation to assume new and greater power. Henceforth, they were to oversee not just the neighborhood efforts taking place in their own cities, villages, and towns, but also to supervise all literacy workers (including all the brigadistas) in their jurisdiction. Closer supervision—and more helpful reinforcement and advice—now came to be routine.

Finally, the government called a National Congress in Havana to assess the basic problems and to determine whether the measures named above could meet the need. With 860,000 people still illiterate and with close to three fourths of the year already gone, there seemed no option but to reach for still more sweeping tactics. Although it was not stated in these terms, a sense of operating on a "war footing" now became explicit in all areas of the campaign.

First, beginning on September 18, participation on the part of the teachers of Cuba ceased to be voluntary. A teacher's draft began that day—applicable to all who had not volunteered, including those at primary, elementary, and secondary levels. One direct result was to postpone the start of school from early September until the beginning of January.

The government's willingness to take this drastic step is evidence of its single-minded concentration on the literacy goal. It also demonstrates that, even in the face of lack of total solidarity within the Left itself in Cuba's government at the time, the leaders felt sufficient confidence in popular support to launch a policy that might well have infuriated thousands of the mothers and the fathers of young kids.

Second, a new idea, "Acceleration Camps," was put into effect across the country, under the direct control of the Municipal Education Councils. Wherever a large number of people had fallen behind in their study of the primer, a team of expert educators, brigadistas, and experienced "People's Teachers" would group together to operate a camp in which *all* of their students—workers, farmers, older neighbors, men and women—would spend entire days in academic labor while others would take their places on the farm or in the working center. The Acceleration Camps appear, by the statistics, to have had phenomenal results.

Third, by the use of car pools, bus service, or whatever, thousands of People's Teachers now went out, day after day, into nearby rural areas that could be reached from major cities, first to recruit, then to instruct, those campesinos whom the brigadistas had not yet been able to identify, to motivate, or teach.

Finally—among the most effective of the step-up tactics—a new kind of pedagogic personnel, "Study Coaches," suddenly appeared. The "Study Coaches" were selected from among the most successful literacy workers and given an accelerated course in utilization of the primer and the manual. There were perhaps no more than several hundred, but their expertise, inventive energy, and intensive training in the fall of 1961 rendered them forceful and effective catalysts wherever they appeared.

The government sent them where they were most desperately needed: into isolated regions where the brigadistas had encountered obstacles of pupil-hesitation, pupil-resistance, or their own inadequacies as teenage teachers. (The Study Coaches paid their own way, both for travel and for living costs.)

By late October the sum total of these efforts at last began to show numerical results. Whereas the exam-completion figure for late August had been not quite 120,000, the figure two months later was 354,000. After an additional two months of unceasing pressure, the total of those who had completed their exams was over 700,000. Although the victory was not yet statistically complete—and would not be for several years to come —Cuba's triumph in the eradication of illiteracy already exceeded anything that has to this day been achieved by any other nation in the world.

In the face of this remarkable event a number of insistent questions will be asked by those who are accustomed to smooth-running programs with non-hectic resolutions:

(1) Why were all of those acceleration measures put off until the fall? Why didn't the Cuban leaders recognize the dangers by the end of June, instead of two months later? The answer, I believe, must be connected with the pace of the campaign. The last of the brigadistas still were finishing up their training courses at the start of August. Not until then did government leaders have a chance to ascertain how well the first young brigadistas had made out.

(2) Why did there have to be so much chaotic interruption of all other areas of life? The answer here will not suffice for those who still adhere to liberal options in a well-fed democratic land. The truth is that in a time of revolution there is no midpoint between *win* and *lose*. The primer had promised, "We Shall Overcome." Cuba could not afford to say, "We tried our best, but did *not* overcome. Next year, all things being favorable, we might well try again . . ." To lose the struggle, at a point when Cuba still was under siege, would have been to compromise the heart and pulse-beat of the revolution in itself.

(3) Why did there have to be so much alarm, so much exhortation, even at last something so harsh and drastic as a draft of teachers? The answer, again, is that the

campaign had been organized in military terms that cor-
responded to the military dangers that the nation faced.
When organizational errors were observed, or when it
was discovered that a single group (the brigadistas, in
this case) could not keep up with the expectations of the
state, immediate self-examination and correction were
essential, even if this meant a short-term period of ur-
gency and pressure.

Those who wonder whether it was possibly unjust to
close down elementary schools in Cuba for the final
months of one year and the autumn of the next in order
to guarantee a triumph in a separate area of national
objectives ought to consider first the massive increase in
the school enrollment (double the prerevolutionary number in the elementary schools alone by 1961). The same
critics then should visit in the elementary and secondary
schools of Cuba of the present day. It would be hard, I
think, to come to the conclusion that the kids in school
in 1961, or those in school today, have been short-
changed.

In order for the literacy campaign to have succeeded
as it did—beyond the expectations of either sympathetic
allies or distrustful viewers from abroad—government
leaders were compelled to draw upon all possible resources, to do so without hesitation and without re-
morse.

In the words of Raúl Ferrer, a man who knows the
painful truth of this, perhaps, the best of all: "We
needed all the people in the wheel of one great task. We
had no choice. In the long run almost every man and
woman answered to the call."

By late October the entire nation had been mobilized
—from the poorest neighborhoods of old Havana to the
smallest mountain villages of Oriente and Las Villas. A
slogan seen on posters almost everywhere encapsulated

the whole sense of heightened rhythm that Ferrer later recalled: "Those who know, teach. Those who don't, learn." TV and radio hammered home the theme: "Every Cuban a teacher, every house a school."

From the first days of the literacy campaign, instructors had been asked to start each session with a new non-literate pupil by filling out a questionnaire that summarized the learner's work-career (present job, place of work, hours, and such) and sought specific details in regard to previous years of formal education, trying also to discover whether the learner could already read a little or else not at all. The instructor was asked to keep a record of the pupil's progress by administration of a series of three tests, the last one to be given only after the completion of the primer.*

More important than the three tests, and certainly a great deal more poetic, was one final bit of evidence that was asked of every person who had learned to read and write. This final evidence was a letter to Fidel, telling him of the consequences of those many nights and days of work. (Those who wrote these letters received in return a textbook that had been prepared to offer further work and, in a sense, to keep alive the spirit of the Great Campaign—even before the organizers had begun the first stage of the Follow-Up.) Seven hundred thousand of these letters are on file in a number of thick albums in the Literacy Museum.

It is self-evident that any government that so desires, can shelve its scruples and solicit testimonials to satisfy its public needs. Those, like myself, who have had the opportunity to study hundreds of these letters without haste in the quiet of the garden in the museum in Havana are forced to judge their spontaneity and au-

*All of these tests and questionnaires may be examined in translation in APPENDIX.

thenticity by personal reactions. My own instinct, despite some uniformity in tone and choice of words, is to accept them as the open manifestations of both pride and personal liberation on the part of newly educated men and women:

El Ingle, 14 June 1961
Dr. Fidel Castro
Prime Minister

I am making these few lines for you so as to tell you that I didn't know how to read or write and thanks to you, who put the literacy campaign into practice, and to the teachers that are teaching me, I can already read and write. I am a member of the militia and I work in the Rogelio Perea Cooperative and I would like you to come to this cooperative.

Viva la revolución socialista
Patria o Muerte
Venceremos
Yours truly,
Felix D. Pereira Hernández

November 14, 1961
Year of Education
Comrade Fidel Castro:

I am very thankful because I know how to write and read. I would like you to send me the Follow-Up books to improve my knowledge more in the reading and in the writing. To be an educated people is to be free.

Your comrade,
Domingo Franco Mesa
Venceremos!

After the last non-literate member of a family had passed the last exam and had completed the handwritten letter to Fidel, a flag went up above the doorway of the house: "Territorio Libre de Analfabetismo." The flag, often made of paper, was almost entirely red, with a small book open to the letter A in its upper left-hand corner as a symbol of the competence which now had been achieved.

When the last house in a town, village, or neighborhood within a major city had put up that flag above the door, the town (or neighborhood) itself was privileged to fly the flag. A friendly competition soon evolved among the various provinces of Cuba in order to determine which one could claim the credit for the first municipality to fly that flag.

The first town in all of Cuba to deserve the right to fly the flag turned out to be a village in Havana Province called "Melena del Sur." As the records of examinations and official compilations show, the town was declared "Territorio Libre de Analfabetismo" at twelve noon, November 5, 1961.

Seven weeks later, on December 22, Cuba itself—a nation dotted now with several hundred thousand paper flags of literate men and women—was declared by Fidel Castro to be "Territory Free from Illiteracy." The claim does not exceed the reasonable limits of poetic license.

The most authoritative documentation of the literacy struggle, the one report compiled shortly after the campaign, is the UNESCO bulletin, researched during 1964 and published one year later. The report renders the final compilation in these terms:

According to the latest census taken prior to the revolution, 23.6 percent of Cuban adults were illiterate. The number of illiterates diminished slightly during the advance of the revolutionary army through the villages of Oriente during 1956, 1957, and 1958. A more substantial

decrease in the number of illiterates is attributed to a
period of experimental programs during 1959 and 1960.
Simultaneously, the vast improvement and redoubled
enrollment of the public schools served to reduce still
more the number of non-literate adults. (Estimates suggest that the illiteracy rate, by early 1961, had already
been reduced to twenty percent.)

By the start of 1961, the Education Ministry had established 979,207 as a working-figure for non-literates
in Cuba. Of this number, 707,212 were taught to read in
less than nine months. Two hundred seventy-two thousand partial illiterates remained—out of an adult population which, in 1962, was close to five and a half million.
In percentile terms this means that less than five percent of Cuba's population still remained illiterate. No
other Latin American nation had ever brought the
figure for non-readers to a point as low as eight percent.
The Latin American median, as of 1960, was 32.5 percent. An exact figure for the United States—then or now
—is difficult to pin down. UNESCO, however (1973),
places it at 6.6 percent, while *The New York Times* has
pegged it three times higher, at a minimum of twenty
percent.

As the Cuban population has grown, subsequent programs and the effectiveness of public elementary
schools have reduced the number of non-literate adults
to a figure of less than two percent. Most of the people
represented by this figure are the sick, the aged, and
those Cubans whose sole language remains Haitian.

The inclination to defuse the Cuban victory or to un-
dermine its meaning or its worth seems to be relentless
among those who cannot bear to give due credit to a
social order that they either dislike or distrust. A common criticism heard among such individuals in the
United States is that human nature is not normally con-

ducive to the kind of hard work carried out by Cuba's "Literacy Army" during 1961. Only coercion, they say, could have brought such massive and exuberant response.

The possibility that human nature may be susceptible to transformation by the moral and emotional climate of a social order is not given credence in these observations. Individual self-interest is taken as the absolute, unalterable characteristic of all men and women on this earth. (Altruistic motivations are attributed only to peculiar persons.) This kind of criticism brooks no rational answer. If there *is* an answer, it seems to me to be self-evident in many of the stories that we have just heard.

Sensitive commentators, on the other hand, have pointed to one major qualification that cannot be treated lightly in any retrospective observation of the Cuban struggle and the pedagogic value of its first results. This is the critical issue of the minimal level of effective reading skills which Cuban educators first defined and then sought to attain.

There is no question but that first- or second-grade competence cannot be significant (i.e., functional, and likely to survive) unless it is closely followed by an ardent effort to raise levels from this marginal competence to one which represents, at very least, a fourth-grade level.

Anything less than this limits the learner to simplistic news, block-letter headlines, non-educative (e.g., exhortatory) posters, simple instructions and directions for machines—but provides no access to sophisticated news analysis, complicated technological instructions, serious essays, difficult verse, sensitive fiction, or the like.

The Great Campaign of 1961, in simple truth, did not achieve, because it did not aspire to, these goals. It did enable 707,000 adults to read posters, poems, and songs written and distributed specifically for their use—and to comprehend the rudiments of the front page of a paper geared to their extremely modest competence.

Cuban leaders recognize today that nothing that was achieved during 1961 would have been of lasting value, in purely pedagogic terms, had it not been for the Follow-Up *(Seguimiento)* which was able to involve in formal academic work at least 500,000 of the 707,000 people who had passed their last exam during 1961.

After a brief period of testing—of experimentation with some sample texts and of selected pilot programs in eight sample areas—the Follow-Up became, in effect, an on-going struggle in the daily life of Cuban men and women. From the *Seguimiento,* it was only one step further to the Battle for the Sixth Grade, which dominates the billboards and the press even today. (Half-a-million adults were able to qualify for this important threshold level by the end of 1968.) As one leaves the city of Havana for the airport, a giant billboard tells the passerby: "THE BATTLE FOR THE SIXTH GRADE IS A BATTLE FOR US ALL."

There was, without question, a very cautious definition given to the word "literacy" right from the start. It is true, as well, that there was a temporary fall-off from the high pitch of national commitment and official propaganda to sustain the fervor and momentum in the early months of 1962. (Statistics, available in the UNESCO bulletin, demonstrate that there was considerable fluctuation in adult-enrollment figures even as late as April 1963.) As a result the nation may have lost some of the initial spark of motivation in a certain number of those campesinos who had shown the highest possible motivation during 1961. It was by no means a case of losing all that had been won—but rather of leaving too much time between the efforts of those energetic volunteers of

1961 and the full-scale institutionalization of the Farmer-Worker Education programs which are now in operation at a high gear.

David Harman, Israeli literacy expert and recent Harvard scholar, strongly agrees with the initial point established here: The Cuban definition of a basic literacy skill was far too low to prove significant as a pedagogic victory in itself. "To bring the issue right back home to the United States," Harman observed in a conversation during 1976, "anyone here whose competence is less than tenth-grade level cannot be viewed as literate in the United States. The definition must be adapted both to the needs of individuals and to the present status of the nation if the word is to mean anything at all.

"From this perspective," Harman said, "twenty-two percent of U.S. citizens cannot do reading at a functional level. An additional thirty-two percent can do so only at a level I consider marginal. I am not speaking, therefore, in specific condemnation of the Cuban effort. It is a simple truth, however, that what Cuba attained—within the boundaries of the single year of 1961—was minimal in the context of the nation's needs. Only when Cuba proves to the world that it has won the Battle for the Sixth Grade will the promise of Fidel have been fulfilled."

Today, the Battle for the Sixth Grade is nearing its completion and emphasis has shifted to the secondary level. In a population which, by 1976, had grown beyond nine million people, six hundred thousand workers, campesinos, merchant seamen, and others were actively involved in academic programs that would lead to either ninth-grade or else twelfth-grade qualification. In all of Cuba's six large universities, which presently enroll more than one hundred twenty thousand pupils, forty-eight percent are active workers, enrolled in regular programs, "orientated courses," or night classes.

Statistics of this kind, however, have a way of drawing our attention off to large abstractions. The real conclusion of the literacy struggle was not in its statistics but in the massive rally that took place in Revolution Square in Cuba on December 22, 1961. Ninety-five thousand student brigadistas and many of their teacher-mentors marched into the center of Havana beneath huge flags and banners that proclaimed their sense of victory and pride. In place of the banner, *Venceremos,* under which they had set forth eight months before, the brigadistas marched under a banner that proclaimed the *past* tense of the verb, *¡Vencimos!* ("We HAVE overcome!")

The march began assembling just as the sun came up at six A.M. Five hundred brigadistas were selected to walk behind the flag of the campaign, each with book and lantern, each one wearing the insignia (CB) of the brigade. Five thousand additional brigadistas followed, walking in rows of twenty-four abreast. They marched into the Revolution Square wearing their tattered olive-colored jackets and berets, many shouldering hammocks, others wearing knapsacks, some swinging their lanterns, others carrying their books. They carried gigantic pencils molded from paper as symbolic substitutes for guns. It took four hours for the long procession to come to its end.

Well past midday Fidel began to speak. Fifteen months before, he had stood at the rostrum of the U.N. General Assembly in New York and told the world what Cuba was prepared to risk, in terms of pride and world esteem, in order to turn back the tide of ignorance within its land.

During the rally members of the youth brigades began to chant: "Fidel! Fidel! What else have we to do?"

Fidel replied in words that brought the literacy campaign to its official end. "Now you must return to school," he said. "When you are done, send me a telegram and tell me that you want a scholarship to go to the university. There you will gain the further skills our people need."

That day the Cuban government began a policy of scholarships for all ninety-five thousand members of the youth brigades. In subsequent months, as Cuba grew into a full-scale socialist state, the scholarship plan was broadened to include all people who could prove their competence and earnest desire for university admission.

There is one postscript to the end of the campaign.

During the weeks that followed, thousands of newly educated campesinos were invited to Havana by the parents of their former teachers. The goal was to establish permanent friendships and (for the parents) to show their gratitude for love and kindness given to their sons and daughters in the previous eight months. But the symbolic meaning of those friendships far transcended any simple demonstration of parental thanks. The joining-together of the city and the country was the starting point of an entirely new phenomenon in Cuban life.

V

The Story of Christina

She sits across the table from me in a small and comfortable room. With us are two of my close friends and an older woman whom I do not know. There is also a photographer.

She is small and slender, fragile in appearance, extremely beautiful in a theatrical way. I mention her beauty because it becomes a major undercurrent in the story that she tells.

Today Christina is thirty-three years old. On January 1, 1961, when she was not yet seventeen, she traveled to Havana with a family which had previously employed her in their home near Santiago, having hired her directly from her father, an impoverished campesino. The precise nature of her status in the home of her employers did not come out in our conversation and I did not ask. A number of the statements that she made, however, seemed to suggest that she was often under pressure to provide more services than the standard duties of domestic labor.

A drastic clash was probably inevitable that year. In spite of her appearance of fragility Christina had been working in the urban underground—as part of a group that formed a network of support for Fidel and the other guerrillas who had established their first stronghold in the mountains near her parents' home in Oriente.

"I had met Frank País, one of the first martyrs—the organizer of the urban underground. He lived close to my family in Santiago. Even though I was still so young, with scarcely any school at all, I had been given a small task to do—to transfer mail and certain parcels that were headed for the soldiers in the hills nearby."

Now, in Havana, two years after the triumph of the revolution, Christina was no longer willing to accept the kind of treatment she had taken in the past. As soon as the literacy campaign was announced, she grew excited at the opportunity.

"One night I came into the house of my employer. I was very happy and I did not wish to cover up my feelings. I said: 'I am going to learn to read and I am going to learn to write.'

"They said that my services would not be needed any more. It was the same night that they put me out."

I asked how close she had been to them up to that time.

"They never really knew me," she replied. "I was a servant. He was a salesman. She was a French woman. I did the work, took both their children off to school, washed and ironed, cooked, and cleaned the woodwork and the floors. The mother had an easy life. She woke up late. She always asked me for a cup of coffee in her bed. It was milk and coffee that she meant."

For all of this they had paid her fifteen pesos [at that time approximately fifteen dollars] every month. It was, quite clearly, not the loss of that particular job that troubled her. It was simply that she had no money, had no family—at least, none closer than five hundred miles, at the other end of Cuba—and no place to go.

"My father couldn't send me money anyway," she said. "The awful thing was that I couldn't even write to *tell* my mother and my father of the trouble I was in. This was the worst. They couldn't read. I couldn't write. Nobody in our family ever had gone to school. I was alone. I left the house of my employer. I went to the place where the reading class was held. I looked in the window from the sidewalk—it was right at the same level as the street—and I saw that the class already had begun. I was very nervous, but I went into the room and sat down in the class. I was in tears, but I was determined that I *had* to learn to read and learn to write."

As she spoke, reliving that night, she struggled not to cry. I asked her if she could recall the substance of the work she did during the next weeks in that class.

"The primer," she said, "is all that I remember now. When we read *Venceremos,* it was very real to me. We learned to understand our own position through the lessons and the pictures. I remember the first lesson on the OEA. The blockade by the U.S. was a serious hardship at the time. It was supported by the OEA." She added: "But, it had one good effect. I think it forced us to grow up."

"After the campaign was over, did you go on with your studies? Or did you feel the wish to lead a normal life and to find useful work?"

"To study," she said, "to learn to read and write, did not seem to be separate from a normal life. The first thing I did, after I had sent my letter to Fidel, was to begin to memorize my favorite poems. This is a habit that I learned during that year. I do it still today . . .

"Then I joined the first program of classes of the Follow-Up. I kept up with my studies, until I had completed the full program of the EOC [The Battle for the

Sixth Grade]. Once I had attained the sixth-grade level and had been given my diploma, I began to do the secondary level. This year I am in the first year of the FOC [ninth-grade equivalence]." She laughed. "Don't ask me, please, what I will do next after that! Maybe I will study next to be a journalist. Then I can go to the United States and question *you* . . ."

In one more effort to recapture the last details of the Great Campaign, I asked Christina if she still remembered the exams she took to prove that she could read and write.

"I can't remember all the details now," she said. "I remember that I learned to write my mother's and my father's names for the first time, but I do not know if that was a part of my exam. I learned the word *revolución* and I learned to write my own name for the first time, too. Everything else, up to the present day, was easy after that . . ."

At this moment the older woman who had come with her spoke out. She said to me: "Perhaps you wonder who I am and why it is that I am here. I am a teacher, a certified teacher—forty-three years in all in public schools. I had answered to the call for People's Teachers when the call went out in 1961. I never dreamed of all the things that would take place within myself as a result.

"It was that night, it was into my small classroom right here, right in this section of Havana, that this woman came in tears to ask me only for the little gift to teach her how to read and how to write.

"She was the brightest student I had ever known. She learned the primer in two months. I didn't know how she found her way into our class, but all of us could sense immediately that she was in great pain. I spoke with her. She told me her employers would not let her come into our class to read and write. The family wanted to go out at night. She had to choose to leave or stay.

"Then, also, I was scared to see her all alone—and it was night. She is a beautiful woman and the old ways had not died away. I was afraid. We were fighting against prostitution at the time. I did not want her to be left without a home. After the class I took her by the hand and we sat down to be alone. She cried her heart out in my arms. I told her I would take her to *my* home. I said that she would be my daughter. I would be her mother."

There was a pause, and then she said: "Now she is married, and so I am a grandmother as well. I would like to tell you that the revolution brought some very deep and very moving changes to our lives. Who would have thought, when Fidel said that 'all who know should teach and all who don't should learn,' that I would receive a daughter, and grandchild, as my first reward?"

Christina went on to speak for a while about her subsequent career. "It had been my dream to study art, but I was married soon, and then there came the babies. Once they were old enough to be enrolled in day-care centers, I went outside the house to find some work. Now I am working as a cashier in a supermarket. I am responsible also for working certain hours in the office of the CDR."

Since I did not know a lot about the CDR (Committees for Defense of the Revolution) other than the fact that these committees had been first established with the primary goal of state security, I asked Christina what she did within the organization.

"I have been responsible for *vigilancia*," she said. "This year, I was promoted to the leadership of *vigilancia* for twenty-one units of the CDR. In this position, I am responsible as well for working in coordination with the municipal police."

I asked if this meant that she was trained to carry arms.

"No," she said. "I have not ever touched a gun."

I asked if she was not a part of the militia.

"All Cuban women are part of the militia. Ever since 1960 all of us have been prepared to go on active duty in the case of an alert. But there are many other things to learn about than how to fire a gun. In my responsibility for the CDR I am concerned with health care of young children, with the problems of old people also, with the pap test, and the other tests for cancer. I am responsible also for the ration cards and for sick people who are all alone and for young women, maybe women like myself when I first walked into that class in 1961, young women who are not aware of their own rights and obligations . . ."

In a curious moment of shy hesitation overcome by an enormous sense of pride, she said: "I am also a vanguard worker in my supermarket." Then, following one final pause: "It seems that a great deal has happened in my life in fifteen years. I hope I have not bored you with the things that I have tried to say . . ."

I asked Christina's former teacher for a bit of background information on the methods she had first employed.

"I already knew of poverty," she said. "I had been a teacher in a fishing village and had seen the terrible suffering before. I used to have one hundred children in one classroom when I taught first grade. They had to sit on the floor; we had no desks or chairs. I used to follow a thin path along the swampy section twice each day, first to get to school, then to get back.

"That was under Batista. Everybody was corrupt. I brought charges against the chairman of the local school board. He had taken the money for the children's breakfast food. It was a famous trial. Later on I was given a more difficult and distant job . . .

"After the revolution, as one of the People's Teachers, I used to read together with my class, then ask one of the students to attempt to read alone. It was not one-to-one, but it was six or seven or eight. After the first few lessons we did writing too. We had been trained to do our work by people who had been a part of the initial team that had composed the primer . . ."

I tried to turn the conversation toward Christina once again. I asked her about the role of women in the years after the triumph of the revolution. She spoke about the well-known film *Lucia*, which she had originally followed on TV. The final portion of that three-part film told the bitter truth of many men who had opposed the liberation of their wives or lovers in the literacy campaign. "Now, in Cuba, there is a Family Code that guarantees the equal rights of women in their homes. Everything is not different in a single day, but it has made a difference for us all. The day-care centers also help us to develop our careers. My daughters are students in the public schools. The little one goes to a day school. My older daughter is a student at a school *en campo* [a five-day boarding school in the country, optional now for junior high school pupils]."

I asked Christina if there had been difficulties during 1961 when Fidel said the schools would not reopen in September.

"No," she said. "There were no difficulties for most people that I knew. People believed that Fidel had come not to deceive us but to defend and educate the poor. All of us had heard about his speech at the Moncada. It was entitled 'History Will Absolve Me.' I am sure that you have heard of it by now."

She spoke one final time about the family she had worked for in Havana: "That family—I never saw them again. Not as a family. I say it like this because it is the truth that one day I did see the head of the family, but not with his wife. It was years later, and I was at my working center. He asked, 'How are you doing?' I said, 'I am an educated woman now, but if I had never left your house, I would never have learned to read and write. It was lucky for me to leave your house! If not, I would have been a maid forever.' He was quiet, but he said that he was glad."

"Was he sincere?"

"I do not think he was sincere," she said. "I think he liked me better as his servant." After a moment's hesitation: "I never knew what happened to them after that. It's possible they went to the United States. If it is so, then I feel sorry for them. They are missing out on something very great—something that they could have helped to shape. Maybe, at least, she has her cup of coffee every day . . ."

My last questions had to do, in a general way, with the tenor of the life she leads today.

"Besides our jobs," she said, "we each have many responsibilities in the revolution." I noticed again, as often before during these conversations, that when I asked a series of questions to an individual person, the answers first would come back in the first person singular but then would frequently wander into the first person plural. I also noticed that people who spoke about their obligations as a citizen today in Cuba, tended—like Christina—not to say that they felt obligations *to* but rather *in* the revolution. It marked the difference between an entity of which they felt themselves to be a part, and one to which they felt subservient, external, or just simply grateful.

"We have to train ourselves in various ways, both in our homes and in our public lives: to keep updated, for example, on international events. Therefore, we meet in political circles and we read political books. We read books that are important to the revolution—Fidel's speeches, the newest program of the CDR, Raúl Castro's speeches in regard to the armed forces . . . We also have read about historical events, important dates and people in our lives . . . Che and Tania . . . poetry too . . . That is still my favorite part . . ."

I asked Christina how she found the time to read a book of verse with all the other things she had to do.

"When you love something, you find time to do it. I still love poetry, so I commit to memory the poetry that I love best. I have memorized 'January First,' 'The Morning of Santana' (it is a poem about Moncada), 'The Story of The Revolutionary Teacher . . .' My favorite poets are Nicolás Guillén, Navarro Luna, and José Martí . . .

"You don't need to be somebody special to enjoy good poetry and music. Culture is important to our way of thinking about life. We do not need it in order to run a factory," she said, *"but we do need it just the same.*

"My two girls like poetry and music also. My older daughter won a prize in ballet. I am her mother, but I think that I can say that she does very, very well in the ballet. She would like to dance, and she is taking lessons for that reason. In spite of this, I think that she prefers another kind of work for her career. My younger child is in the Pioneers.

"All of these things that I have tried to say, all that I love—poetry, music, study, or ballet—all of this goes back, in my own life, to the work we did in 1961. But we have seen many other great events as well: agrarian reform, rent reductions, the building of new schools . . ."

I interrupted to ask about the rent she paid; she had said "reduction" and not "cancellations," whereas I had read before I left for Cuba that all rents were free.

"No," she said, "we do pay rent if we are living in one of the new, post-revolutionary houses. If they are old houses from before the revolution, most of the tenants have by now achieved the right to own their house by paying their rent for five years in a row. For my apartment I do pay rent—although it is extremely small."

She sat in silence for a moment. Then she said: "Without the literacy struggle none of this, of course, would have been possible in my own generation. None of these things—a new apartment, a job I can count on, my daughters in their new schools, an afternoon at the museums . . . music . . . and ballet . . .

"But then, of course, if there had been no revolution, there could not have been a Great Campaign. So all our work and all of our lives go back into the first years of the revolution, back to Moncada, back to the Escambray."

"It goes back into history—into the past," I said, without taking much care to choose my words.

"History is not behind us," she replied. "It does not disappear and go away 'into the past.' It is alive among us still. It is the things we do—and things we say."

My conversation with Christina was only one of several that I had with men and women who first learned to read and write in 1961. Many of the conversations were less poignant and dramatic. There were others that were a great deal more spectacular in terms of the academic opportunities and better economic situations that came within reach as a direct result of new-found literacy skills.

I have talked, for instance, with a woman who is now a school director with full responsibility for the training of two hundred teachers of dressmakers every year. Before the revolution she had never been to school, could neither read nor write; she could not even spell her name in January 1961. The economic and professional transformation of the illiterate daughter of a washer-woman and a dock-worker (as she described herself to me), whose only competence was that she knew the way to use a needle and a piece of thread, into a school director at the age of fifty-four is probably a more important form of evidence of the tremendous impact of a single year of all-out national struggle than the more unusual story of Christina.

There are stories, too, of men and women who now hold important government positions, who are directors of their working centers, or who have become physicians, architects, and such—who could not read or write in 1961. I have heard these recollections not in structured settings but in situations which allowed no possible supervision or intimidation, and from people who could have had no cause to give a false impression to a visiting writer, nor any reason to expect a recompense from someone in the apparatus of the Cuban state. They spoke to me, I feel, with no other motive than their satisfaction, pride, and self-respect.

In the face of a number of stories of this kind, I chose to tell the one I did because it seems to crystallize so many different (and desirable) consequences of a social revolution: freedom from the literal and back-bending servitude of domestic labor; freedom from the likelihood of sexual degradation; freedom from ignorance of advantageous opportunities; freedom from ignorance of her own rights as a citizen and human being; freedom from poverty and hopelessness; freedom even from the inability to write a letter to inform her parents that she was *not* free.

I was moved by the permanence of the love that had grown up between Christina and her teacher—and by those dreams that are at last within her reach and that of her two children, whether those children choose to find work in a factory or to run one, whether they choose to give their lives to art . . . or to ballet . . .

"History is not behind us," she had said. Her words seemed to echo many writings of Fidel and Che: "It is alive among us still. It is the things we do—and things we say."

VI
An Intellectual Embargo

Those many readers who have no reason to be familiar with the history of adult literacy work may very well be curious to know whether Cuba's efforts took place in a vacuum or whether similar projects were (or had been) underway in other nations.

The only other major adult literacy efforts to have taken place since 1950 were those attempted by UNESCO. (Smaller programs have been attempted by some church groups and by AID—but all with minimal success. The only other nation that has tried to launch a major struggle on its own is Mexico. Here, too, the rate of failure was disheartening. Fifty percent remained illiterate)

In 1965 UNESCO first announced a plan to undertake twelve pilot projects and eight "micro" ventures in eighteen Third World nations. Eleven projects were actually attempted; thirty-two million dollars were expended. The result in every case, according to David Harman in a book published during 1974, was almost total failure.

In Algeria, for example, after two years of operation,

a program directed at 100,000 people showed participation by no more than 1,400 pupils. In Mali, of 110,000 would-be pupils, only 20,000 could be found. In Tanzania participation was intended for a quarter-million adults; the figure never came close to five thousand. H. S. Bhola of UNESCO reported—after a test administered not to pupils in Tanzania but to teachers—that over fifty percent of those who had been hired to teach reading were not effectively literate themselves. In Ethiopia results of another massive program were summarized in simple words by this evaluation from UNESCO: "The entire effort is now considered to [have been] a waste." Similar reports came from Madagascar, Nigeria, Ecuador, Syria, India, and Mali.

The most disturbing part of the whole business is not so much the failure and the waste of scarce resources but rather the apparent effort at deception. In-house evaluations are one matter; official UNESCO publications are another. In three successive papercover volumes on the progress of its efforts *(Literacy 1965, '66, '69)*, UNESCO failed to come out with the fact that nothing it had tried had met with measurable success—and that, in simple truth, it was throwing good money after bad.

Throughout that period funding agencies kept pressing UNESCO for evaluations. UNESCO, to quote one scholar who requested anonymity, "tried to stonewall its complete defeat." A more generous way to say this, possibly, is not that UNESCO sought to hide the truth but that it tried to postpone its full revelation, like Mr. Micawber, in the hope that something good would suddenly "turn up." John Simmons of the World Bank, meanwhile, took an independent look at what was going on in Madagascar and Algeria. In his report he pointed out that *not one pupil* had learned to read in either program.

At last, in 1976, in an official publication *(The Experi-*

mental World Literacy Programme: A Critical Assessment), UNESCO virtually conceded that it had just wasted thirty-two million dollars. UNESCO, of course, did not use a word like "wasted" in its publication but some of its representatives could find no other term to designate the truth. In the words of Schwana Tropp, spokesperson for UNESCO in New York, the program was "a startling and shocking waste in almost all respects."

What had gone wrong?

"It is," said David Harman in the course of the lengthy interview he granted to me in Cambridge, Mass., in 1976, "the same point that the Cuban educators recognized right from the start. Education of adult illiterates without some parallel form of socio-economic transformation is unthinkable. It *has* to be accompanied by food and land and health care and the rest. Without these items no endeavor of this kind has ever yet achieved even a marginal success."

In this regard the initial reaction of UNESCO to the Cuban struggle was bizarre, to say the very least. During the nineteen sixties UNESCO recognized that it might be of use to study the campaign in Cuba. One of the individuals assigned to carry out the work was the Italian scholar Dr. Anna Lorenzetto. Dr. Lorenzetto's on-site study of the Cuban struggle, including interviews with several of the same men and women I first met in 1976, was published in 1965. Printed in English, French, and Spanish, Dr. Lorenzetto's study is a strong, enthusiastic comment on the literacy campaign, giving full recognition to the ideological bias of the primer and the militant preparation of the brigadistas.

Dr. Lorenzetto handles the military parallel not just with openness but with a note of positive endorsement. She does not condemn the Cuban people for responding to a state of siege with siege mentality and siege precautions. Her full report, although officially in print since

CHILDREN OF THE REVOLUTION

1965 and listed by UNESCO in New York and Paris, has not been readily available through UNESCO for ten years. A condensation of Dr. Lorenzetto's views, however, was published in 1968 in the magazine *Convergence,* released by the Ontario Institute.

The problem, as far as UNESCO was concerned, seems all too clear: The only major literacy program of the nineteen sixties which had *not* been funded by UNESCO was the only one that proved to be a real success. In the words of David Harman, UNESCO's subsequent behavior represents "an international scandal."

The report, he said, was much too good. It made the efforts of UNESCO look too bad. Therefore, UNESCO had to undercut or else divert attention from the work of Dr. Lorenzetto. The solution was the ultimate in circumvention: not to refute Dr. Lorenzetto's work, not to dispute the triumph of the Cuban undertaking, not even to send a second, possibly more cautious team to check things out again, but simply to suppress the work of Dr. Lorenzetto altogether—or, at least, as best it could.

David Harman's observations are of special interest here. Though clearly anti-Castro in his politics, he is an even-minded and discerning man. He also is honest in the tribute that he pays.

"Everywhere else but Cuba, adult literacy campaigns of every kind have always failed," he told me in the course of our discussion at his home in Cambridge. Harman explained the previous efforts in this field in terms of three distinct historic phases. "First, there was the classic missionary phase, initiated by a man named Laubach. He originally tried out a program in the Philippines. It failed to show results but Laubach did a brilliant job of self-promotion. Naturally, his book was soon translated into several hundred languages so that every other nation could fail also.

"Laubach's is a ludicrous and hopeless method: 'A for

airplane . . . Z for zoo . . .' All of this gets memorized and instantly forgotten. Laubach is dead by now, I think. He has a son who carries on his work . . .

"The next phase was the one identified with Lenin— a method of adult education developed in the early period of the Soviet state. This was really no more than an ideological adaptation of the Christian missionary goal: 'We must have literate adults, not in this case to read Gospel but in order to read technical manuals and political posters, in order to be effective partisans of the socialist state.'"

Lenin's program began in 1921. Twenty years later, in 1941, Stalin proclaimed an end to all adult illiteracy. His claim, according to Harman once again, was meaningless:

"The fact is that the public schools of the Soviet Union had been doing an excellent job and had taught those children who were now adults to read while they were still in school. This had nothing to do with Lenin's adult literacy program. It isn't a special insult to the U.S.S.R. It is the norm among such literacy programs.

"A third approach to adult education," in the words of Harman, "is described as 'education for modernization' . . . 'education for self-realization' . . . something of that kind. The goal, as in all modern nations, is a heightened technological capacity. In approach, of course, it is 'nonpolitical' and, in ideological respects, it might be labeled 'antiseptic.' Gunnar Myrdal seems to have invested confidence in methods very close to this. I regard this also as a sham.

"There is only one approach that I find credible. It cuts through all the talk of methods, gimmicks, gadgets, and the like and gets to the real point. It is very well described in Tolstoi's book *On Education*. He poses the standard questions and he gives us a good answer: 'Do we begin with word-sounds or with full-word identifications?' The point is: It doesn't matter either way. None of it works, in any case, unless it is allied with something else. That 'something else' is what they did in Cuba. It is the promise of a better life for every man and woman in the land—and parallel actions which confirm to the participants that this indeed will be the case. This is precisely what UNESCO does not dare to do —and doubtless never will. It is the reason why UNESCO's money makes no difference. It is the reason why UNESCO always fails . . .

"During those campaigns financed by UNESCO, the likelihood of failure was predictable. Eighty percent of those who came dropped out before the programs were complete. Of those who stuck it out, fifty percent lost what they had learned within a single year. At best, if we are kind and optimistic, we can say that ten percent of those involved might have held on to something they had learned.

"For all of these reasons, Cuba—which has turned its back upon the safe and mechanistic methods of UNESCO —must be given credit for a triumph which is totally unique.

"Cuba, in few words, has created a new culture and (I hope this doesn't sound too fancy) has been able to accelerate the pace of ethical evolution . . . No honorable scholar, in the face of all that Cuba has achieved, can claim the right to denigrate its scope, its sweeping energy, and ultimate worth to all the rest of us who have tried so hard but have repeatedly come up with so much less."

UNESCO did not publish Dr. Lorenzetto's work. Cuba was forced to publish her report at its own cost. UNESCO never even bothered to explain its own behavior. Instead, it kept a limited number of copies of the Lorenzetto work in its bookstalls or its resource areas in Paris and New York and did not take the trouble to replenish the supply when these were gone. It also rejected a request by Cuba that a number of copies of the document be made available to scholars at the worldwide literacy conference which it organized in Teheran in 1965.

Dr. Ferrer, a member of the Cuban delegation to that conference, anticipated an exclusion of this kind. He therefore brought with him five hundred copies of the Lorenzetto study. As the conference began, he stood by the doorway of the auditorium and passed the booklet out to every delegation that arrived.

"Have you seen this yet?" he said. "It's very interesting reading from my point of view."

"How is it interesting?" he was asked.

"It seems that the Cubans have been teaching adults how to read and write with good results for four or five years now, since 1961, while we here at UNESCO have been having such a disappointing time."

"How do you know this?" he was asked.

"I've read it in this study by UNESCO," said Ferrer, as he handed a copy to each person who passed by. "Why don't you read it too?"

In the face of criticism so severe, and emanating from such well-respected sources, I did what I could to get a thoughtful statement from UNESCO. I wrote a letter to the Deputy Director-General, John Fobes.

Mr. Fobes in his reply to me spoke without evasion of the fact that the UNESCO document of 1976 failed to make any reference, even in passing, to the startling success of Cuba's parallel endeavor. He attributed this to "a variety of reasons." One of them, as he conceded, was that adult programs of this sort rely upon financial aid "from sources which insist on evidence of economic (industrial) returns . . ."

In other words, he was blunt enough to say—or to suggest—the international interests that support

UNESCO's unsuccessful projects might not like to be reminded of a very different kind of project: one that *works*, and works, in part, by such unprecedented methods as the simultaneous expropriation of both land and factories of foreign corporations . . .

In regard to Cuba's charge that the report of Dr. Lorenzetto was denied appropriate publication by UNESCO, Mr. Fobes replied that the report was given to the Cuban Ministry of Education for Cuba's use in publication, adding that this "is the case with most such missions." For all his candor he fails to explain why the unique success reported in this document did not compel those in UNESCO who have some serious *interest* in success to make an exception and to publish the report themselves. "Business as usual" is the heart of Mr. Fobes's reply. But the Cuban venture was not usual business. This is the point on which UNESCO's whole position falls apart.

Clearly, it would not be fair to pin the previous failures of UNESCO on one person: in this case, a straightforward man who, speaking for himself, has nothing but praise for Cuba's obvious achievement. He praises the courage that Cuba displayed and also suggests that many other nations doubtless wish that they could come up with the same results. Mr. Fobes (who is regarded with considerable respect by Raúl Ferrer) appears to be a diligent and honest man, stuck with the task of trying to defend a series of unfortunate events that were not, and are not now, his own responsibility.

The real problem is the old familiar syndrome of the type of project that UNESCO chose to undertake in the beginning: the same kind of project that is carried out so frequently both in the U.S. and in Europe, not to "win a battle" but to "test out an idea." (So long as we can designate our project an "experiment," then clearly there can be no charge of failure.) All of this would be quite fine, of course—and harmless, too—if millions of people did not starve and live in ignorance as a direct result.

The reader may be curious by now to find out what it was precisely in the Lorenzetto research that provoked so many people to so much discomfort and confusion at UNESCO. What is it that UNESCO took such pains to undercut, to slight or else "transcend"?

"When an illiterate adult," Dr. Lorenzetto has written, "starts on a course to learn . . . to read and write, society itself [begins to] go to school. . . . The school opens its doors to life experiences, work problems, the tragedy of poverty. Society goes to school, and learns . . . to read and write; this process can release unknown forces . . ." Some of these forces, she says, prove to be "dangerous."

This, she goes on, is the only possible explanation of that strange state of affairs by which the adult education programs fostered by UNESCO prove, every time, to be increasingly restricted to those areas of content and concern that never really count—issues that do not stir the heart and cannot motivate the soul.

The words and views quoted and paraphrased above are taken from the essay Dr. Lorenzetto published in *Convergence* in September 1968. In 1965, however (in her original report), Dr. Lorenzetto worded the same point in even sharper terms:

"If the [present] evaluation of this Campaign, which was a great event in the educational field, cannot be set apart from a political evaluation, this is due to the fact that the Campaign was, in itself, a political event. The very results of the Literacy Campaign, which were unquestionably positive, cannot be perfectly understood in the educational field, without taking into consideration the social and cultural objectives . . .

"People's participation and a consciousness of the so-

cial and economic realities continue to be the basic post-
ulates of all work to abolish illiteracy . . ."

Dr. Lorenzetto ends her commentary on the Cuban
struggle with a note of optimism and good cheer. She
mentions, first, that cautious elements in Cuba (and
some of those watching from the outside, too) suggested at the start a three-year rather than a one-year
program.

"It was possible," she says, "that the illiterate could
wait three years . . . The revolution could not . . .

"It is possible that, in three years, the . . . campesino
could have learned how to read and write by means of
the radio, television and technical . . . procedures." But
he would not have gained a political consciousness
thereby. Thanks to the efforts of the youth brigades, she
writes, the campesino has learned not only how to read
and write but also to become a revolutionary.

"As we have already pointed out," she says," the post-
literacy work will shortly begin . . . It is a problem as
important for Cuba, in the present day, as the struggle
against illiteracy was in 1961, a problem whose solution,
through the efforts of Farmer-Worker education, should
[soon] provide the total population with a sixth grade
educational level."

The confidence of Dr. Lorenzetto in Cuba's capability
and will to carry out a powerful follow-up proved jus-
tified. It is one of several points at which she demonstrates a realistic faith in Cuban claims and Cuban resolutions which those who were her supervisors at UNESCO
did not seem to share . . .

All institutions, fortunately, are not equally immune
to self-examination. Some, like UNESCO, change more
rapidly than most. UNESCO today is by no means the
upper-class neo-colonial club that it resembled back in
1965.

One obvious evidence of a new posture at UNESCO in

regard to Cuba's work is a small book for students of
the same age as the Cuban brigadistas (See NOTES for
this and other recent publications of UNESCO)—a book in
which the author, praising student activism in all sections of the world, elevates the Cuban work of 1961 to
an exalted role. The literacy campaign, he says, was not
just a triumphant struggle by a youthful population.
Rather, speaking of the multiple programs that were
rapidly set up by the Cuban leaders, in order to guarantee continuation of the work of 1961, it is "a success
story that has no end . . ."

Dr. Ferrer tends in conversation to diminish his own
role in the literacy struggle, yet it is Ferrer more than
any other person who today remains most active and
most energetic in support of those programs that have
carried on the spirit of the Great Campaign.

In the course of a conversation with Ferrer and his
close friend of many years, Abel Prieto Morales—soldier, organizer, teacher, and former Minister of Elementary Education—a conversation that began at ten A.M.
and ended with both men still going strong at ten past
six, Ferrer spoke of the literacy efforts that have taken
place in several other nations of the Third World.

He pointed to UNESCO projects in Algeria, Tanzania,
India, the Sudan, Mali, Madagascar . . . "Why do they
fail?" he asked. "They have the money. They have the
expertise. They have the international promotion. They
have UNESCO. How is it possible, then, that they do not
succeed?"

"It is because their starting-point is anti-human. It is
because they do not dare to use the words we use. They
do not dare to speak of land reform, to speak about the
sick and starving . . . nor about the ones who *make* those
people sick and poor . . . the North American corporations and the banks . . . They do not dare to put these

words into the hands of the poor people. And, because they do not dare, therefore they fail—*and they will always fail until they do!*"

He stormed at me in pouring out these words. For just a moment I believe that I had come to represent for him all of those institutions that he had just named and obviously despised. Ferrer's distinguished but somewhat more dispassionate colleague, sitting at his side, said to me in perfect English, "Do not be alarmed. It is his helpless loss of self-control. Raúl is growing old . . ."

The laughter between them, old and loyal friends, helped to cool the atmosphere and we went on.

I asked Ferrer, in view of his last words, if politics must in every case be tied to education for a program of this kind to work.

He answered by speaking of the almost physical relationship between the campesino and "the word." A man, he said, ". . . in order to feel that he can be the owner of the *word* . . . must sense that he can also be the owner of REAL THINGS. I mean, the owner of his own existence, of his toil, of the fruit of his own work. In order to sense that it can be within his power to possess the *word*, he must believe that he can thereby gain the power to transform the *world* . . . to shape the world . . . to make it a more noble and more humane place to be . . . There is no way to do this which is not political."

Prieto interrupted briefly to recall the story of a conversation he had held with several European educators some years earlier in Rome. " 'Is it true,' I was asked, 'that the schools in Cuba serve the interests of the state?' I replied: 'Of course they do—just as they did before the revolution, and just as they do today in France and Italy and in every other modern nation that I know.' It is remarkable to me that so many people still attempt to fool themselves about a point so obvious and clear. All education is political in one respect or other. There is no way to perpetrate the myth that education can be neutral."

Ferrer spoke next about a phrase in popular use in the United States in recent years: the "crisis" in the schools. "Ever since the student upheavals in Paris during May of 1968 hundreds of people have been traveling the world in an attempt to isolate the crisis of our pupils from the moral struggles of our times. It is a gross diversion. We deny that there is 'a crisis in the schools.' We believe the so-called crisis in the schools emerges from the struggle of young people to remake society. It is not a crisis in the classroom. It is a crisis in the social order."

Suddenly now, without attempting to pursue a rigid sequence of whatever kind, Dr. Ferrer went on to speak of six or seven different and wide-ranging issues. Much of what he said seemed to flow forth in a single wave. In actual fact there were a number of brief interruptions, marked by an assistant bringing in a tray of juice, by Dr. Ferrer removing the wrapper from a long cigar and slowly clipping off the end, by various comments too (largely at Ferrer's expense) from his old friend, who sat almost the whole day in mock-stoic silence at his side.

"The literacy campaign," Ferrer announced, "was not a dry event. It must not be talked about as if it were. It was passionate, turbulent, sometimes desperate—but, above all, it was a political event.

"The statistics of the end results are very good. Yet this was not at any time our chief concern. This fact was a by-product of a deeper goal. The great heart of the literacy struggle was the revolution. Its chief result: a farmer-worker-student coalition. Above all else the students in the cities learned the greatest lesson of their lives: *reading* that 'book of life' not from a printed text but from the campesinos whom they were assigned to teach. There is perhaps a kind of poetry in this. If so, it is a poetry that is not mine. The poetry is there already in the history of the campaign."

He paused a moment, drew on his cigar and then went on. "Fidel said to us once that we had made a revolution bigger than ourselves. He was correct, yet very few people in the world have knowledge of the things that we achieved. Why is this so?

"One reason, of course, is that we all have worked so hard; we did not have the time at first to sit down and to publish our results. Then, too, there was the embargo from outside. The real blockade was not the one that planted U.S. naval craft around our shores. The one that hurt the most was intellectual. The great embargo was to silence the results of our campaign.

"People assumed, 'All other struggles in the field of literacy fail. Then so must this one too . . .' "

Prieto attempted to explain to me the reference, which at that time I did not yet understand: "In 1964 UNESCO had sent an excellent scholar, Anna Lorenzetto, to report on our campaign. Lorenzetto, it seems, became a great deal too enthusiastic. UNESCO refused to publish her report unless she would agree to censor certain passages and phrases.

"We told UNESCO, 'You have permission to edit a document that you can publish, but you must not cut away materials that will subvert the passion and enthusiasm.' The book, in the final event, was never published by UNESCO. We had to publish it ourselves.

"You will have heard perhaps already of the subsequent confrontation in Iran. Raúl Ferrer stood by the door. He held in his hands five hundred copies, printed in English, French, and Spanish—and he passed them out. It was as if he were a newsboy in New York. In seven minutes every copy that he had was gone."

The smile suddenly vanished from his eyes. "I would

like to ask you to imagine the indignity of this . . . not
so much for my good friend beside me here as for the
Cuban people as a whole. How do you think a nation—
no matter how small, or poor, or powerless—would
feel?"

Ferrer leaned back within his chair, looked down into
his hands for a moment, and then spoke these words:

"Of course, all that is part of history. UNESCO has
changed a great deal in the course of ten or twelve
years. Now it shows much better taste. As a matter of
record I have the proof right here."

As he spoke, he first inscribed, then handed to me, a
copy of his own new book on adult education. "It is
published here in Havana, but it gets wide distribution
from UNESCO. So you see, their taste must have improved a great deal in ten years!" He laughed at his
own words, then added: "Times change. We need to
speak the truth and then we need to set aside the past.
UNESCO is a different animal today from what it was
before . . ."

Without warning, Ferrer took off in an entirely new
direction. "Illiteracy, of course, is not an absolute idea.
It is forever relative. Our approach, therefore, must
change as need demands. In 1961 our definition of a
literate man or woman was a person who could understand some plain and simple words. It was like starting
up a car and moving into gear. The Follow-Up and Battle
for the Sixth Grade were the subsequent gears. In the
beginning, as you know, the campesinos studied words
like 'INRA' and 'tierra' . . . 'analfabetismo' . . . 'OEA.'
Today, after sixteen years of work, we are making use
of an entirely different set of words."

I asked him, when I had a chance to interrupt,
whether there was nothing other than the words themselves which he would change if he were starting back
again in 1961.

"No theoretical change would seem appropriate," he said. "Organizational patterns would be watched with greater care. Challenges that we did not face before the end of the summer would be dealt with earlier in the year. These are mechanical matters which we would, of course, attempt to fix. We would not want to make the same mistakes again that we have made before. No reversal of theoretical goals, however, would take place. Social motivation would not change.

"The active words, the generative themes, these are the things that we would alter with the years. We would not speak today of 'INRA' and of 'OEA.' They are no longer vitalizing words. We would speak instead of mechanized ways of bringing in the crop, of fibers, coffee production, polyclinics, or hydraulic systems. We would speak perhaps about Che's letter to Fidel, the children of Vietnam, and the struggle of the Cuban women for their equal rights . . .

"In each generation new words are released and old words fade away. Today we would be speaking about irrigation, popular power, citrus groves, and the tobacco crop. Sometimes I listen to a man I knew before the revolution. He speaks now of the nickel export, schools-in-the-country, or the Cuban fishing fleet. I listen and I find it isn't the same man! Why would a peasant need to speak of citrus crops before the revolution? What did the peasant woman have to say of citrus crops? We did not *have* a citrus crop in Cuba!"

Ferrer stopped to give his patient friend a chance to speak. "It is correct, of course, we did not have a citrus crop," Prieto said. "Yet there are many other changes in the active language of the people too. My son, who is only five years old, hears me speaking of a time when blacks and whites were not allowed to dance together. He asks me why, but when I tell him that it is because of 'racist' views, he does not know that word. He says it is 'ridiculous,' not racist. The whole idea does not make sense! He does not understand that there was once a time when 'racist' was a necessary word in our land. We needed it in order to describe a real phenomenon—one that does not exist except in isolated situations anymore."

With scarcely a pause, Ferrer went on to speak of an entirely different point:

"In regard to the so-called silence of the poor—you have heard us speak of this before, but there is one more thing I need to say. The vegetable Indian in some little town of Mexico or Guatemala . . . He is a silent man. He does not speak . . . But put into his hands a revolution —he will begin to talk! He *is* a 'vegetable.' I said it! Yes! It is the perfect word—*because he has been rooted in that soil for so long!*"

He drew on that cigar (his third or fourth) a final time, then pressed it out, and went on to elaborate on his idea of "vegetable silence" and the sudden rediscovery, by a man who was oppressed, of his own voice:

"Those who oppressed us, those who denied us, those who took away our voice of protest—when they were finished, they had married us to the lie. So long as we were not free men, we were compelled to live in company with that lie. The world crumbles when a people choose to live no longer with a lie.

"When do we free ourselves from the power of that lie? We free ourselves not when we announce that we are free but when we bring about events that *make* us free. A man no longer lives with the lie when he no longer will accept to live in a subjected role."

Prieto interrupted briefly at this point. It was in a voice of fragile strength, surprising to me, in view of his demeanor and impressive eyes. "There is a certain beauty in those words that makes it possible to cry. Yet you must understand"—he paused to make the impact of his statement more direct by looking straight into my eyes—"that those are not the words of Raúl Ferrer. They are from a speech delivered several years ago by Dr. Castro. Those lines have great importance in our consciousness of life and pain. It is the truth: When we disown that lie, the world of the oppressor will collapse forever."

Ferrer began again. "I want to speak of something else which I have not defined explicitly up to this time. Perhaps you wonder what our ultimate objective possibly could be—perhaps you don't! Whether you do or not, I want to speak of this again. It is a crucial point. The original objective was political awareness—plus minimal competence for productive needs. In the early days our primers were like weapons. Our enemy was illiteracy every bit as much as the embargo of the U.S.A. Today our goal is not just minimal competence and a basic consciousness of military danger as before. It is the richness and the resonance of culture, solidarity with people in the other socialist lands, a heightened capability to deal with high technology and middle-level expertise. We could not even dream of goals like these before . . .

"What will be the end result of all these undertakings? When society functions right, the nation itself becomes an all-embracing school. Education is everywhere. Fidel once said that Cuba is a giant school."

Ferrer spoke for a while about the adult education programs and the motivations needed for a worker to assume the added burden of a rigorous evening program, in addition to the obligations of his daily work. Then he began to laugh, and while I waited for an explanation, he began to recollect the story of a man who had no serious ideological direction—nor the slightest interest in political concerns:

"The man said: 'I want to learn to write.' We asked

him why. He said: 'So I can write a letter to the woman that I love.' He came into the program and—I'll tell you something—*that man learned to read and write extremely fast.* When he was done, he wrote a letter to the woman that he loved: 'I write one thing that I long to tell you. Inside my body are many fearful things I need to say. Cruel woman, if you do not love me, I will die.' "

Ferrer smiled. "Many people memorized those words. They were transcribed into a popular verse and later set to music by a good songwriter. The trouble is—his woman didn't love him! But he didn't die. He met another woman he liked better! Still, it is a good poem—even better as a song."

Ferrer laughed again. "And so you see—everything we do is not political. Most things are, but writing-motivation takes a thousand forms. Who would have thought of setting up a primer to enable campesinos to write letters to the man or woman that they love?"

He seemed to enjoy the memory immensely. "But there you are. He didn't give a damn about redistribution of the land. He wanted to write a letter to the woman that he loved. Then she had the nerve to turn him down. So he went on to find somebody else. Now he is a semi-skilled mechanic in Las Villas. He is a happy man, as we are told. It seems that now, in middle age, he has become a little more committed to the struggles of the state."

It was late afternoon. I began to be concerned that I would miss my chance to ask a question that I still considered basic to the whole discussion. Ferrer, however, would not let up on the topic of the agonies of love. He turned the conversation suddenly to me:

"I understand that you are hopelessly in love . . . Is the young woman committed to the same ideals as you?"

I said she was, in my belief, a great deal more commit-

ted than I to a socialist ideal. I told him she had wept as
the Cubana plane set down upon the landing-strip and
as the airport sign came into view.

"Why is it, then, she did not come with you to visit us
today? We would have liked to know her as our friend,
as we are coming to know you."

I explained that she had been obliged to go back to the
U.S. two weeks earlier, in order not to lose a job that she
had worked hard to obtain.

Ferrer looked at Prieto, as if he were prepared to
spring a trap—and wanted Prieto's approval first. He
asked me then, "How long have you known each other?"

I told him that we had met only five months before.

"Then this must be a painful time for you . . . She is
in Boston . . . You are in Havana . . . It is all so sad . . ."

Ferrer was smiling broadly now. "Did you know that
I write poetry and songs?"

I said that I did not.

Prieto (in English): "He writes the songs . . . *so bad!*"

Ferrer (in English also): "I write . . . *so good* the songs
—and I write *very good* the poetry too. Would you like
to see a little book I wrote? I also love to sing. I can play
for you on the guitar."

Prieto: "No!"

Ferrer (in English): "I sing also my own songs. I can
sing one of my songs right now if everybody likes."

By now Prieto had developed an amusing look of anguish on his face. It was clear, no matter what Prieto
said, that we were in for a concert on the part of Raúl
Ferrer. He went behind his desk and came back with an
old guitar. For six or seven minutes, Dr. Prieto, former
Chief of Staff for Adult Education in the Revolutionary
Army of the West, along with a delighted and admiring
translator and a deeply moved (and totally disarmed)
reporter from the U.S.A. listened to the songs of love
that had been written by Ferrer.

Months later I came upon one of his songs, published as a poem in a papercover book prepared for use by Cuban adults working "to achieve the sixth grade."

Ferrer at last put down his old guitar, told me his song had been intended to be dedicated to the woman that I loved, and asked again how long it would be before we hoped to meet. I said I would be flying home in five more days.

Ferrer smiled, positioned his hands, palm facing palm, about three feet apart. "When you meet her, it will be like . . . *so!*" He brought his hands together with a crash: "It will be—two locomotives in the night." Martha laughed before she would agree to tell me what he said.

"In any case I want to toast your happiness with a little glass."

He poured from a decanter four small glasses of some kind of blackberry brandy I had never seen before.

"No politics," said Prieto. "Please!"

Ferrer lifted his glass, held it to me—then drank it in one gulp. The atmosphere in the room was gentle and relaxed. I wondered if any other country in the world had ever had an adult education minister quite like Ferrer.

After that discursion I did not know how to get back to the final question I still had to ask. Dr. Prieto recognized the situation and assisted me by asking if I had some final inquiries to make.

I said there was one further question.

Ferrer sat straight up in his chair. "I am ready to listen. Ask me anything you want."

My question seemed so dry, I hardly had the nerve to ask it now. I explained to Dr. Ferrer that I had been asked by a newspaper editor in the United States to find out what the literacy program cost in terms of hard investment, cash, diversion of resources to a single goal:

budget, costs and "fiscal trade-off" in the jargon of the educational planning experts in New York.

"In Cuba," he replied, as calm and level-headed as if there had been no laughter, no music, no liqueur, "there can be no balance sheet for justice. We know, of course, that Cuba spent so many million pesos to produce the primer and the manual. Then Fidel issued severe instructions in regard to health and safety of the brigadistas and in reference to their means of transportation to the places they were sent to work. Some went by bus. Some went by special train. We know the cost was great. It is a cost, moreover, that was shared by local villages and towns. I do not think that we could ever make a proper compilation of that cost.

"Speaking still of money, not humanity, the largest cost of all was what each family paid whenever a son or daughter went to work in one of the brigades. I mean the dual expense both to support some of the child's costs while living in the mountains and the farms and also to go out to visit now and then—and to bring food, because the family in the country was so poor.

"I can give no figure. But I can tell you that millions of pesos were expended in the early phase of the campaign. One hundred seventy-seven thousand pairs of glasses had to be produced and fitted to each person who had need for glasses. You have heard this already, but it was not *just* the cost to buy the glasses; technicians also had to move into the villages to fit the glasses. Then, too, doctors had to go into the country, as you know, to offer health care to the brigadistas. Do you see how many different kinds of cost we had to face? It was not just the teaching of reading as a technical idea. It was a concert written by the forces of a total people. The Rebel Youth, the Federation of Cuban Woman, each of them made their own investment too. One hundred twenty-seven separate towns

93

and cities made financial contributions. Each one had its own responsibilities.

"The salaries of the professional teachers represented another cost as well. From May to December thirty-five thousand teachers were given their conventional pay to work as guides and as advisors to the brigadistas. Ninety-five thousand lanterns, uniforms, knapsacks, hammocks, had to be obtained.

"Then you must recall, as well, that we had not declared ourselves a socialist nation at the time that the campaign began. We did so *during* the campaign, but in the interim we still had private enterprise in Cuba. So that made it doubly hard.

"What, then, is the total? We can quantify the salaries of teachers. We can add up the production loss caused by workers who joined the brigadistas during September when it seemed that we might fall behind our goal. But we cannot quantify the salaries of those—the People's Teachers, the ordinary men and women of the land —who gave up two or three hours every day in order to share their reading skills with neighbors. How can you quantify this kind of cost?"

We had been talking now for almost an entire day. Ferrer leaned forward, placed his hand over my wrist, and then went on.

"We must disappoint your editor," he said, "but we will send that man an answer, all the same. It is precisely this: If you must always count up everything in numbers and must forever calculate the cost in dollars, you do not succeed, and never *will* succeed, in struggles of this kind.

"The treasure of the Third World is the treasure of our people, not their cash. We do not deny the necessity of money, but in these kinds of struggles the real price is something that cannot be put in numbers."

It was past six o'clock. I watched the energy and passion of this man whom Paulo Freire had described to me three months before in Canada as "a great tree of life."

Prieto, silent now, impressive and almost austere—ascetic in his silence—did not smile any longer but looked with admiration at his longtime friend.

I asked Dr. Ferrer: "Do you ever stop to rest? When do you ever get a chance to eat?"

His eyes were shining with nostalgia and exhilaration: "The literacy campaign was one of the great moments —one of the immortal moments—in our history and in our lives. We count on you to tell our story right."

Part Two

The Battle for the Sixth Grade

(For Cuban Adults the Follow-Up Goes On)

I

In all of the enthusiasm for the education of the young, it must be apparent also by this point that Cuba has not turned its back on those adults who worked their hearts out in the Great Campaign and in the Follow-Up programs of the subsequent ten years.

Dr. Ferrer concedes that there was one brief period of temporary slow-down and delay in getting the adult programs underway, immediately after the triumph of the Great Campaign. Ferrer, however, attributes this delay to the time required for preparation of new teachers and of new materials. He refers, for example, to the preparation of a series of new pamphlets bridging the gap from *Venceremos* to the Battle for the Sixth Grade. The series was distributed throughout the country, free of charge, in fixed installments every fifteen days. (At that stage the government still was trying to establish guidelines and to determine the best organizational structure for the total plan.)

Today it is self-evident that the adult program is meticulous and comprehensive in its organization and its guiding policies. The basic breakdown of the program looks like this:

Those who are working to achieve the sixth-grade level are participants in that portion of the plan which is called the "EOC"—letters that stand for "Worker-Farmer Education" (Educación Obrera/Campesina). Over three hundred thousand adult men and women were enrolled in courses of the EOC in 1975. The government hopes to see the final wrap-up ("triumph") of the Battle for the Sixth Grade by the end of 1980.

The adult program at the "lower-secondary" level is known as "FOC" (Facultad Obrera/Campesina). It corresponds exactly with the level of the junior high. Approximately one hundred twenty-five thousand people—peasants and workers—are enrolled in classes of the FOC. The government hopes, in this case, to "achieve the victory" (i.e., to establish ninth-grade competence as a *uniform minimal skill* throughout the nation) by 1982. In this instance, I suspect that government expectations are too high. If the first goal is to win the Battle for the Sixth Grade by the end of 1980, it is not easy to believe a ninth-grade level can be reached in only two years more. A realistic goal might be some time soon after 1985.

At the high-school level adults are enrolled in what is basically the "third stage" of the program. It is called the "CSSO" (Secondary Course of Worker Self-Improvement) and it leads to the exact equivalent of twelfth grade. There are several other, smaller programs too: one for those who wish to gain a mastery of foreign languages, one for those who wish to become teachers. The present figure for *all* citizens enrolled in adult education programs is above six hundred thousand. In total numbers, since the end of 1961, two million adults have been graduated from one or another of these plans.

Since the Cuban population has increased so much since 1961, it may not prove a lot to render compilations in the form of absolute numbers. A better index is to use percentiles. To take the sixth-grade level on its own, eighty percent of Cuban adults still had not achieved that competence in 1963. By 1974, however, forty percent at most fell short of the sixth grade. (As we have seen, the government hopes to see this forty percent reduced to zero in the next two years.)

One matter that repeatedly perplexes me whenever I examine figures and statistics of this kind is the question of apportionment of time. The schedule of hours that the government has charted out for something like six hundred thousand workers and farmers seems to add up to a total that is slightly past belief: eight hours in the working center (factory or farm), three hours in formal classes every night, three hours for meals, two hours for transportation, one more hour frequently for block meetings, party meetings, or the like. Adding it up once while I was in Cuba, I calculated that there were at most seven free and unencumbered hours in a day in which a citizen might have a beer, read a magazine, visit with friends, see a movie, play with a child, spend time alone with someone that one loves—or just catch up on sleep.

In answer to my question teachers and organizers told me they had struggled with this problem now for several years. "The study week," said one of the organizers of the EOC, "was first established as a full five days. It was too much for the workers to sustain. Today it is reduced to four. Wednesday is left free for relaxation or to go to meetings. Saturday is free from classes, too. Sunday is free from work and classes both. In addition the working centers now provide a lower workload, at the same pay, to accommodate the students in their ranks. In the same vein teachers in the classrooms have been asked to cut down on the pace of academic obligations.

"There is, however, something which you still must understand. No matter how hard we try to make the work less hectic, less exhausting, less severe, nonetheless there is the realistic fact that Cuba is a nation with a mania for productivity today. The nation is desperate for maximum production. Most of us have learned to live on a far smaller allocation of free time, of sleep, of rest, than would be common in a nation like your own. In our belief this is what it takes to build a revolution. Citizens who are strong, and not disabled, *have* to work—and we need women too. We could not do it if the women did not form an equal portion of the labor-force . . .

"Still," he said, swinging back to emphasize the other side once more, "for all our work and productivity, you cannot help but notice that the concerts held on Sunday afternoons are full. The theaters are crowded. The beaches and the public pools are crowded too. The movie-houses and the cabarets are full . . ."

This is the truth and it would not be accurate to suggest that Cuban citizens, for all the emphasis on "work and school," have given up the normal pleasures of a buoyant and—on weekends certainly, in both Havana and a number of much smaller cities, villages and towns that I have seen—a truly contagious sense of energy and fun. The long lines in front of stores, the ration cards, and other forms of deprivation do not seem to dampen the high spirits of most people that one meets, even though shortages, lines, and all the rest are clearly inconvenient and cannot be talked away.

Always, and everywhere, it must be said once more, people are *reading*. They are reading books, both foreign and domestic. They are reading newspapers, pamphlets, magazines. They are reading while they stand in line, sit on buses, wait for a train. It is a phenomenon for almost any North American, or possibly for any foreigner, to see. It is this—this seemingly obsessive wish to read, to write, to learn, to *know*, and then to read and write some more—it is this, above all, that I had come to Cuba to attempt to understand.

II

My understanding grew a great deal deeper one day in September 1976 when I walked into the office of a woman named Rosario García. By definition, I suppose, Dr. García must be designated as a "bureaucrat," in the literal sense that she directs the lower-secondary level of the adult education plan: the FOC. She holds moreover, a position of immense responsibility, as we have seen—with almost one hundred twenty-five thousand adults now involved in an increasingly sophisticated program that will double or triple in enrollment, if present projections hold, within the next five years.

In part, for just this reason, I went to our interview with expectations of a crisp, efficient, and statistics-spouting organizer—the director of a costly, sprawling, and enormously ambitious educational campaign. Instead, to my delight, I met one of the most explosive, non-statistical, unconventional human dynamos of any government or nation—socialist or not—in any city of this earth.

As I think of her now, I am reminded once again of many of those stories told about La Pasionaria, the legendary spirit of the anti-Franco forces in the Spanish Civil War. A solid, four-square, highly intelligent woman, maybe fifty-five years of age, Rosario García sits at her desk and looks out at her visitor from under beetling brows, through clear blue eyes that fire up with indignation at the smallest possible excuse.

"I am General Secretary of the Communist Party in the Vice-Ministry of Adult Education," she announced to me right at the start. "Our goal, above all else, is to create a revolutionary consciousness among the men and women of our adult schools. Simultaneous with this purpose is the goal of educating people in a series of sequential, formal education programs, conceived as preparation for a high degree of technological expertise, while giving support as well to many local neighborhood programs which endeavor to educate the people in such basic matters as the care of children, infant psychology, the need for pap tests and for other means of early recognition of the signs of cancer.

"Two groups, in reality, have the obligation to fulfill these roles: the Committees for Defense of the Revolution [CDR] and the Federation of Cuban Women [FMC.]

"Together, they can reach into all neighborhoods of Cuba, since CDR's exist in every block and every little town. If an elderly person, for example, is not seen out on the street for several days, it is the obligation of the CDR to go upstairs into that person's home and to find out if he or she is incapacitated somehow.

"The CDR and FMC work in close cooperation with the Ministry of Health. Proper prenatal care depends upon the use of polyclinics, but polyclinics can be of no use to anyone if women do not recognize the need to keep appointments. Therefore, we rely upon the CDR and FMC. As soon as a woman is pregnant it is her obligation to go to the nearest polyclinic. The patient sees the same nurse or same doctor every time. If a woman fails to show up for appointments, someone from the CDR goes to her home and tries to find out what has prevented her from keeping the appointment.

"We consider good prenatal care a privilege, but an obligation too. A woman, once she is pregnant, is required to attend a series of prenatal lessons. The lessons deal with natural childbirth, breathing-exercises, and the like. If she does not go, someone will go to her house and find the reason why . . .

"All of this, of course, is not—strictly speaking—part of our formal plan of adult education. My colleagues have been briefing you on several of these plans. For now I want to speak of certain other things that come to mind."

After many days of statistical briefings—valuable, but often repetitive, and sometimes dull—I was reassured to learn that she, as well as I, should prove to be exhausted by the same statistics. Our dialogue turned instead to certain personal, polemical, and philosophical points that lay at the center of the adult education scheme in Cuba.

"One of the major goals of our entire program," she began, "is not simply that the student gains a concrete body of specific knowledge, then passes an exam to show us what he knows—but rather that each student senses that he is expected to pass on the knowledge he receives to someone else.

"In the early years after the revolution, we would often speak these words, but I am afraid it is the truth that we were thinking mainly of the young, or else of young adults. We would put up posters: "CHILDREN ARE THE REVOLUTION!" It was an exciting slogan, but—to be quite candid—it was lacking in profundity and sensitivity. It also led to certain unfortunate implications in regard to an apparent absence of concern for the creative possibilities of older people. The literacy campaign, for example, kept the focus constantly upon the young. The romantic figures at the center of the stage were, from start to end, the brigadistas.

"We sense today the very great untapped potential of the old, even the very, very old. This is a new development within our consciousness. We want to be certain that we do not sacrifice the useful knowledge of those men and women who have tried so long and worked so hard to bring about a better life within our land. All who know should have the right to teach. We used to say this during 1961, but it is more true in practice for us now. The old can teach the young to plant the seeds and tend the citrus trees, but they can also teach the children how to live with dignity and how to overcome their fear and desperation, moments of panic, and feelings that we are inadequate—those feelings that, at times, afflict us all . . ."

In order to confirm that this concern with older people was not mere rhetoric, but that it had been thoroughly incorporated into the reflective processes that lay beneath the total adult education plan, Dr. García gave me an example of meticulous attention to the motivations of the older pupils:

"You have heard of EOC and FOC and CSSO—every possible sort of beautiful alphabetic combination." She laughed at herself, then emphasized one point: "The titles are real. The programs are authentic. These names, however, have one other function, too. A father does not like to say to his two children, 'I am working for the fourth-grade level . . . I am working for the seventh-grade diploma . . .' Possibly his own two children are already tenth- or twelfth-grade students. How does he feel?

"Besides, it is the truth that he *does* know a great deal

more than either of his kids, even if his knowledge is not verbal. So the words that we use help to spare the father or the mother from a sense of losing face before a daughter or a son. 'I am in EOC,' they will report—not 'I am in first grade.' 'I am in FOC'—not 'I am in junior high . . .' You may not believe this is a serious distinction. In psychological terms, however, it has been of great importance, in my own belief."

She stopped abruptly to show me a text prepared for adult education. In the creation of this book, she said, she had attempted to make contributions.

"We felt it was essential to produce material that would be equal to the moral depth and the imagination of the adult learner—not just a dressed-up version of material for kids. Therefore, we worked very hard in order to produce this book. The book places primary emphasis on technology—since we need this area of expertise, above all else, in order to keep alive our economic growth. Yet it is also essential, in our view, to find the words we use, as much as possible, within the context of the pupil's life.

"Fundamental to the total process is the teacher's sense of challenge in the face of the vocabulary which exists already in the richness of the learner's consciousness. I mean by this the oral vocabulary which already is so rich and so diverse and which transcends the teacher's by a great deal very often. One example, in a farming village, is the agricultural and technological vocabulary. The campesino knows these words. The teacher frequently does *not*. What, then, does the teacher do? She bases her instruction on the knowledge already present in that person she has come to teach. The teacher must be in the situation of providing real instruction, but at the same time of receiving information, too."

Dr. García returned to the theme of "dialogical exchange" and of the kinds of words that would most logically emerge. "I don't want a dead vocabulary!" she repeated several times in a loud voice, at one point knocking over a small glass of pineapple juice beside her hand. "I want a *live* vocabulary! I want an *active* set of nouns! And *active* verbs! I want an *active* set of words."

At that moment the door opened, a secretary entered, handed a small sheet of folded paper to Dr. García, waited while she read it, then—as Dr. García folded it and placed it in a drawer—stepped away, and quietly withdrew. For a minute or two Martha and I sat in silence. Then, frowning a bit as if she had to force herself to get back to the point at hand, Dr. García picked up again on the subject of the search for "active" words and motivating themes:

"We place a great deal of emphasis on major problems that are faced by allies of our nation in the Third World. Issues like Angola and Vietnam are examined and discussed as part of writing lessons. There is no question but that there is an ideological bias in our texts. We do not pretend we do not have a point of view. The adults who participate have strong impressions in their hearts about these issues, too. The exercise of *reading* this material exposes the pupil to the viewpoints of the state, but the exercise of *composition* enables the learner to enter into dialogue with the teacher by setting down his already-rich ideas on paper.

"This dialogical aspect is essential to our pedagogic view. Textbooks for adults must not base themselves upon the kinds of motivation that are present in the textbooks for the young. At this level motivation must originate within the adult world: a person's home, his work, his role as father, husband, citizen . . . then his concern for *other* people who are struggling for liberation too. There are those in certain nations who do not believe that revolution has a place in adult education, but those are the same people, by and large, who do not believe that there is any need for revolution in the first place! On this subject we do not equivocate in Cuba. We are believers in the need for social revolution. I will not try to qualify my words. I am a revolutionary woman. I have been so my whole life . . .

"Then, too, there is the fact that Cuba still lives with a sense of danger from the U.S. military. Each day we read another story of investigations of the CIA. Where do we read it? We read it in *The New York Times!* Not in *Tass*, not in *Humanité*, not in the Cuban press. It is there, in your own paper, that we read the details of the plots to kill our citizens, to assassinate our leaders, to destroy our animals and crops.

"Do you see a little irony in this? If you were a Cuban, and if you read these items in the most distinguished paper of the U.S.A., how would you feel? Would you not feel a little bit of indignation? We sense, therefore, how much we are in danger and we also know we must defend ourselves through solidarity with other socialist lands. This continues to be the case, whatever the President of the U.S.A. or any of his representatives may choose to say—no matter what accommodations we may make with one another in the years ahead . . ."

Dr. García returned to a brief reminiscence of the literacy struggle of fifteen years before:

"All of our present work in adult education derives from the tradition of the work of 1961. It was, as you know by now, a revolutionary high-point in our lives. There is another precedent, however, for the work we do. In 1962, during a speech delivered to a gathering of youth, Che Guevara said it was the right of all young people who had defended Cuba at Playa Girón to enter the universities or any other form of higher education that they might desire. We took the words of Che in a symbolic sense, since many people had contributed in one way or another to the victory at Girón. We took it to mean that all adults who wished to learn should have the chance to study in well organized curricula—leading, if the learner wished, to studies at the university level.

"Therefore, we feel that we can take our mandate from Fidel and Che alike. We do not *need* to find a mandate for all the things we do or say and there are one hundred thousand things I do each week or day for which I do not think that I could possibly find a mandate, even if I took the time to try. In this situation, however, we believe that we are working in a good tradition . . ."

By now the interview was almost over. I asked a few last questions in an effort to recheck a few more details. Martha and I were then escorted to the elevator by Rosario. As we walked along the corridor, she suddenly asked my age. After I answered her, she looked away.

"I have a son," she said at last, "almost as old as you. Tell me one thing that I was wondering during these hours: What will become of you when you go home to the United States? Will they attack you? Will they discredit you? I do not mean because you came to Cuba. Many people from your country make this journey nowadays. I am thinking, rather, of the fact that you have clearly been excited by a number of the programs you have had a chance to see. Will this not be viewed as evidence, right from the start, that you have been manipulated, brainwashed, or deceived by your long conversations with Prieto and Ferrer and with the other teachers and directors you have had an opportunity to meet? There is no way that I can judge these things. I do not meet with many North American young men here in my office on an ordinary Tuesday afternoon . . ."

I told her that I would most certainly not be arrested or attacked, since I had been given legal privilege to visit Cuba. I said, however, that my words and viewpoints would, no doubt, be held up to abuse—and in many cases, by my friends—as socialist propaganda or the product of brainwashing, or the like.

"Everything I write that's good in reference to the Cuban schools will be accused of being just a little bit *too* good. Anything I say that's bad will be accused of being understated. It will be said the 'good' is not so good as I would like to think. It will be said the 'bad' is worse than I could ever know. . . . They will not bother to say I am a liar. They will simply say I am naive—or else inept."

I had missed Dr. García's point. "I am sure," she said, "that you are well-prepared to deal with literary criticism of that kind. I am thinking of *direct* attacks. A scholar we admire named Letelier was blown up in his car today in Washington, D.C., while we were in the midst of our discussion. I was informed of this while we were talking, but I did not want to interrupt. Do you recall the name? Someone else was killed with him, as well . . . a North American woman, I believe . . . It seems you live in a very violent land. I have a feeling of uneasiness, therefore, because I know that you will soon be going home."

At the elevator she pressed my hand with both of hers, then held me in a long *abrazo*, making several of her colleagues stand impatiently and wait. Finally she said to me that I must call her, or else write to her, if I should need additional information in my work. When the elevator doors had closed, Martha appeared unnaturally moved.

"Rosario," she said after a moment, "is a tough and arbitrary woman. You do not get to be the secretary general of a party branch if you are not a strong and militant soul. I have to tell you that I was surprised to see the way she said goodbye to you just now. She has never spoken to a visitor that way."

I told her that it was because Rosario had been thinking of her son.

"No, it has nothing to do with that," she said. "Rosario is not a sentimental woman. She is not naïve. She
is a revolutionary woman. She may not be right to see
things solely in a physical respect, as with Letelier—
retaliation and real terror of that kind. You do not represent sufficient danger to your government to justify this
kind of obvious approach. I differ with Rosario in this.
I believe that in the U.S.A. results like these will be
achieved by methods that involve predominantly economic fear and psychological alarm.

"There are all sorts of ways to break a person down.
Little by little you will feel less confidence, less courage,
less determination to write letters to us, to keep posters
we have given you up on your walls, to stand beside us
in your heart and in your spoken words. Social pressures
will bear down on you. Your publishers will lead you to
feel worried if you say just such and so about our
schools . . . or such and so about the adult classes you
have seen . . .

"Then, at last, your mother and your father will begin
to be alarmed. I have seen the same thing happen six or
seven times by now. A social order that has weapons
such as these has little need to put young men in prison.
What better way to dominate their views and to suppress the 'wrong' ideas of independent minds than to
enmesh a person in a web of terrors and anxieties like
these?"

A driver pulled up to the curb to take us back to the
hotel.

III

The first full-length evening that I spent in visiting the classes of the FOC started as a teacher's seminar, much like the kind I've joined, or organized, in the United States. I asked right off about the range of possible techniques for "stirring up the hot coals" in a class of weary adults—a class that does not even start prior to five P.M.

"Sometimes, at night," one man replied, "a teacher has to shout, jump up in the air, do any goddamn thing to keep the class awake. We do not look for passive types of teachers who are ready to sit back and wait forever until the students in their classes come to life!"

Another teacher pointed out that almost all the students in her class were women: "The average age has lowered in the past few years. The older women have, in large part, passed the level of the sixth grade by this time—or else they feel they are too old and that it is too late to try."

I asked what brought so many people out so late to classes that were often so far from their homes.

"Money is one motivation without question." The answer was straightforward. "Those who can handle more sophisticated work *will* earn a bit more salary each week. I am nonetheless convinced that if this were the single motivation, we would not have such crowded classrooms as we do."

I asked about some of the other motivations.

"The dynamism of the teacher is one obvious motivation. There is, along with this, the direct consequence of propaganda. All the people are encouraged to improve themselves in every way they can. This is the direction that our propaganda takes. The greatest motivation, though, is probably the sense of emulation. Individual incentive is not viewed as contradictory to a collective spirit. It is understood that, in an emulative sense, all personal achievement is respected in collective terms. I hope you understand this point and that I have not been unnecessarily obscure. It is in the long run, in my own view, the greatest single point of difference between our schools and yours . . ."

A bell rang. I took advantage of the interruption to request a visit to one of the English classes. Five minutes later Martha and I were sitting in a class of students ranging in age from seventeen to seventy and working at a level parallel to the ninth grade of the junior high.

I asked the class, in English, how many years they had been studying "my language." The students, relaxed even in the presence of a North American and his friend, answered that they had been learning English for four years.

I asked them how they started out: with written work or by a conversational approach?

"We begin exclusively with oral methods," said one man who looked to be approximately twenty-five. "It is specifically a British method, but the texts we use are published here in Cuba or in Canada."

I asked the same young man what sort of English books he found most interesting. Several voices interrupted to provide an answer, but he overwhelmed the rest: "I don't mind Edgar Allan Poe . . . and also Thackeray . . ." He stopped on Thackeray: "Is he an Englishman?" I said that Thackeray was an English writer. The young man nodded briskly and went on: "To be quite honest with you, I prefer Charles Dickens. He is the English writer that I like the most. *Oliver Twist* . . . *David Copperfield* . . . *The Story of Two Cities* . . . Those are some of the English novels that I like a lot."

I asked about the North American authors. He told me that he liked Mark Twain and Hemingway a lot, but found the paragraphs and sentences of William Faulkner much too hard to follow or enjoy.

I asked if any of the pupils had read Shakespeare. Ten out of two dozen pupils raised their hands, but when I asked them if they liked what they had read, only three hands remained. "It was too hard," one student said, to which the others all agreed.

I found myself impressed that adults, working at the rough equivalent of ninth grade, had even made a stab at Shakespeare. I was especially impressed that, of all British and American authors, Twain and Dickens clearly swept the field.

"When you read North American authors, do you get a bad impression or a good impression of our way of life in the United States?"

"Sometimes good and sometimes bad," replied one twenty-year-old man. "There is more that I dislike than that I like."

"What is it that you don't like?"

"To be quite clear, I do not like the whole American approach to life."

"What do you have in mind when you refer to an American approach to life?"

One student said: "I think of Richard Nixon."

"Now, however, he is not our president. Moreover, we have a new election coming up." It was autumn 1976. "What do you think about the choice before us now?"

At first nobody answered. Then, one student hesitantly spoke: "Jimmy Carter—he was governor of Georgia, I believe. I have heard he has a beautiful house . . . The other one is Gerald Ford. He is the leader of the Grand Old Party. Is that right? The G.O.P.?"

The students, despite my inquiries, did not come up with any clearcut favorite between Ford and Carter. "They seem the same to me," one student said. "They both are paid for by the people who have all the money and who own the largest homes."

I changed the subject to approach the women's issue. "Are you aware of the women's movement in the United States? Women in the U.S. still do not receive an equal chance in getting jobs, promotion or good pay. Can you tell me if it's different here in Cuba?"

The same young man who had been speaking a great deal before this point began to answer. I interrupted to suggest that possibly a woman might prefer to speak, but the women in the group seemed hesitant and shy. I tried my best to coax them to present their own beliefs, but I had no success. The same young man therefore took up the burden once again.

"Well, to be honest, up to now they are *not* equal in the practical sense. They are equal in the legal sense, of course, and they are equal in their opportunity for jobs. We are trying to get everyone together, but it is the truth that we have not yet done all that we can."

When I asked about the sharing of responsibilities at home—cleaning the floor, cooking the food, caring for the kids—he gave me a slightly canned response:

117

"Of course, the babies come from both the man and woman. Each of them should do part of the job. If a woman needs to study or to go to work, then I think her husband needs to help out in the home. The housework should be done by both of them. If not, it isn't fair. But it is only honest to admit that many people do not feel this way."

I was glad he was so honest on the last part—and grateful that the teacher did not try to qualify or edit his remarks. The clearest message, however, remained the silent voices of the women in the class: too shy, too reticent, too well broken by tradition, to reject their age-old "place," or even to stand up and give an answer on a subject so important to their own existence.

Fidel has been emphatic in his criticism of the fact that Cuban women still compose only about one third of the entire work-force of the nation. It will be of interest to see with what success the Cubans can achieve the goal of equal rights for women in the years immediately ahead.

The next night I went to visit another portion of the adult education program, an elementary-level school, "Escuela Puerto Rico Libre."

The school, like many others run by the FOC and EOC, is situated in a crowded house that once was probably the mansion of a wealthy family. The equipment is rough by contrast to the ultramodern structures and equipment offered to the children of the elementary and secondary schools. The house contains eight class-rooms, including a garage which seventeen years ago was probably the sanctuary of a Cadillac or Chevrolet.

Each class has between fifteen and twenty-five pupils. Several classes take place at once and the walls are so thin that it is possible to "audit" several sessions at the same time. The age range is seventeen to seventy. There are two separate sessions every day. Those who work the evening shift come here at two and leave at five P.M. Those who do an ordinary shift come here for the evening sessions which begin at five and end at eight P.M. In toto, the two sessions involve three hundred pupils and approximately fifteen teachers.

I had asked to visit six of the eight classes. In each I noticed that the class began with the taking of a strict attendance record. Two "head teachers" served to maintain supervision while they also did the job of teaching class.

In every classroom, at the top of the rough and antiquated blackboard, I saw the same date: *Año XX*. It was the twentieth year since Fidel Castro's *Granma* expedition had arrived near Santiago, on the southern coast of Oriente.

Students took careful notes in traditional notebooks. The classes were conventional, both in their "look" and in their methodological approach, but they were free, relaxed, irreverent, in a way that I have seldom seen before. The classes I saw were studying these subjects: Biology, Physics, Plane Geometry, English, Spanish Composition, Algebra. The sessions were animated and informal—sometimes even playful.

Teachers frequently gave chalk to pupils and would ask them to come up and help their fellow pupils. In one class, on quadratic equations, I was asked to come up to the blackboard. I went into a mild panic and said, "No, I'd rather watch." A man who looked approximately sixty took up the challenge, went to the board, and scratched out the answer with apparent ease.

I visited next a first-year course in plane geometry. The subject was the calculation of the area of parallelograms. This time I kept hoping for an invitation to participate, but did not receive my chance. A woman with gray hair—forty-five or fifty years of age—went to the board, studied the problem, and solved it. Five other students came up to the blackboard to do several other problems of this kind. Men and women started to chat a bit in the back row; little by little, their discussion grew intrusive. The teacher was a confident woman, although she was extremely young.

"¿Compañeras? ¿Compañeros?"

The class came to a calm, respectful silence. The pupils sat and did their work at one-arm desk tops of a kind I had not seen for fifteen years. For all the heat and noise, there was remarkable attention. Several pupils who came to the board looked over sixty-five. One young woman, sitting beside me, did not look as if she could be over seventeen.

None of the students was distracted by my presence. They listened to their teacher, who was openly assertive and (in U.S. terms) "directive." Clearly, she knew where she was going on this Thursday night in late September 1976. Every lesson, every detail, seemed to be well planned, with an explicit goal.

The bell rang. (Each class lasted from forty-five to fifty minutes.) In the next class, physics, I stayed for almost the entire session. A monitor, not over twenty-one, was leading a special catch-up session. She held up a small model of an old Volkswagen "bug," then used the bug to illustrate a point about inertia. Over the door there was a map of South America with a swastika over the area where Chile ought to be. The monitor reviewed a number of ideas: magnetism, light, momentum, Newton's laws . . .

The men were dressed in slacks and shirts—the women in informal clothes, some in household dresses, others in light jerseys, shirts and slacks. Two or three kids were playing in the kitchen in the back part of the house. The heat and the humidity had pressed my shirt against my skin. I noticed that several men and women now were reaching for their handkerchiefs to mop their brows.

The teacher, a middle-aged man, took over from the monitor. He spoke to the students with an easy charm and great enthusiasm in regard to their up-coming tests. The subject was again inertia. He concluded the session with two rapid, pleasant, and effective lessons.

First, he placed a jar, filled to the top with water, on a sheet of paper and then pulled away the paper with sufficient force that the water did not trickle from the glass. The students seemed impressed, not so much by the magical non-spilling of the glass as by his confidence and smile. He then asked for a student volunteer. A short and heavy-set man stood up, but stayed beside his desk. The teacher politely asked him to come up before the class, then gave him an unexpected shove that sent him to the floor.

"This is momentum when it overcomes inertia."

He helped the student from the floor—and they shook hands. The whole class smiled.

His final questions had to do with measurements: "Can we measure weight, heat, temperature, or volume? Can we measure mass and energy? Electric forces? Or the various forms of radiation? Can we measure loyalty? Or honesty? Or love?"

Until the last three questions he received affirmative answers every time. Now the answers all were given in the form of slowly turning heads: "No . . . We cannot measure loyalty . . . No . . . We cannot measure honesty . . . We cannot measure love . . ."

The bell rang. The class was over for the night. The next day all of these pupils would be working on a farm or in a factory for six, seven, or eight hours prior to the time that they appeared again at this small school of Puerto Rico Libre.

121

The heat and the humidity would doubtless be no easier tomorrow. The weariness of work, the inevitable human worries of three hundred separate lives would be no less. The goals of national growth and strength and self-defense and personal self-improvement would remain.

In all of Cuba more than six hundred thousand men and women are engaged in programs similar to this one every evening, every afternoon, four days a week, for forty-eight weeks a year. The heat in most of the schools is no less great than in the classrooms of Escuela Puerto Rico Libre. The rooms are no less crowded and the dedication of the pupils is no less intense . . .

I arrived in Cuba with many hopes, but almost as many reservations. It was nights like this one in the school of Puerto Rico Libre that persuaded me of human capabilities far greater than I ever had imagined possible—and pedagogic patience and persistence that I never had even dreamed about before.

Part Three

A Long Day's Journey

(A Conversation with the Man Who Runs the Cuban Public Schools)

I

The all-out struggle of the Great Campaign established a pattern that is visible today at almost every level of the Cuban schools. One of the most remarkable demonstrations of the permanent impact of that year is a new development in secondary education, now (in 1978) in its ninth year of operation.

It is a phenomenon known as "schools-in-the-country" —a plan by which almost one half of all the junior high school kids of Cuba will, by 1985, be spending their seventh-, eighth-, and ninth-grade years at one of a thousand five-day boarding-schools which function at the same time as experimental dairies, citrus groves, or ordinary farms.

The schools-in-the-country are often designated by the Cuban leaders as the single most explicit manifestation of a pedagogic principle first expressed in written form almost a century ago in an essay by José Martí. "Ideally," said Martí, "we should not speak of schools at all, but rather we should speak of schools as workshops for real life. In the morning, the pen—but, in the afternoon, the plow." In the deepest sense, it is upon the spirit of these words that all of Cuban education has been based, but in no case quite so clearly as within the schools *en campo.*

I had an opportunity to visit half a dozen of these schools, and to speak with students in the classrooms, in the corridors, and in the fields. I also was able to visit, and at certain times to teach, a number of the English classes. (English is a mandatory second language in the Cuban schools.) I therefore felt I had unusual access, not just to the buildings and the fields, but—most important—to the children who were students in these schools.

Before I give a first-hand presentation of the views and values of those students, and of those who run their schools, it seems to me that readers will be better situated in the longitude and latitude of Cuban education if I can present a rapid summary of just exactly how that schooling system "works," in terms of avenues of pupil-option, avenues of obligation, variations in curriculum, and skills that represent the preconditions for particular careers.

From the time that they are forty-five days old, Cuban children are allowed to enter day-care programs as parents wish or job pressures demand. At six a child enters first grade. Every child goes to elementary school up to completion of the sixth grade and to "lower-level secondary" up to completion of the ninth. At that point the pupil has the right to three additional years which constitute pre-university preparation.

From ninth grade on, however, there are several other options besides *pre-universidad.* Students who wish can go directly from the ninth grade into pedagogic institutes (five years) to achieve certification as school-teachers at the elementary level. Those who wish to qualify as secondary teachers must finish the same three years of lower-level secondary. Then, they too must spend five years in teacher-training schools. (After 1980, the training plan for teachers will be more demanding. Completion of the twelfth grade will become a precondition for admission to the course of preparation for *both* levels.)

Those students who prefer to go directly into polytechnic schools (whether technological, industrial, or agricultural) can do so after the ninth grade—and can complete their qualifications for employment in three years, by the end of what would otherwise have been their last year in *pre-universidad.*

There is at least one other avenue of secondary-level education. This is a continuous six-year program of intensive academic preparation in one of two highly sophisticated "academic cities"—large, sprawling, ultramodern institutions—both of which are viewed as prototypes for the construction of about one dozen more. The two schools of this kind already in operation (Vladimir Lenin and José Martí) carry their pupils from the start of lower-level secondary (seventh grade of junior high) to the last year of *pre-universidad.* Almost all their pupils go to universities.

The freedom to transfer from one of these academic channels to another depends a great deal on grade level and, unquestionably, on the current state of national priorities. In general students are not trapped within a lockstep, leading to a mandated career, prior to the high-school level. Fourteen-year-old boarding pupils in a new school-in-the-country, for example, are not made to feel that they are marked for life as agricultural technologists, animal breeding experts, or the like. After the junior high school stage, however, preferences for particular fields do begin to be equivalent to lifelong choices of career.

127

If, at a future date, the Cuban government achieves the level of technological and economic independence which it cheerfully expects, there will doubtless be a great deal less peer pressure, as well as less pressure from above, to persist in a field of expertise, once undertaken. At present Cuba cannot afford to be so flexible as many of its educators wish.

As to expense: A child's education, from food to clothes and health care, and from day-care to the last semester of a university career, is paid for by the state. There are no private schools in Cuba. The rate of those who attend school, and *remain* there, between the ages of six and sixteen, is 92.2 percent.

In total figures: By 1976, over three million three hundred thousand Cubans—workers, farmers, adults, kids —were enrolled in formal education at some level: one out of three in a population of nine million five hundred thousand people. No other government in the Latin world comes even close.

II

Of all the visits that I made within the Cuban schools, three of the most impressive took place during the same day. That day (October 1, 1976) began with very little warning at approximately nine A.M. I was sitting with Martha Acosta in the lobby of my hotel—planning together a quiet and unhurried morning devoted to a careful reexamination of some of those items that had particularly intrigued me in the Literacy Museum.

Instead, while we were making plans and as I was fitting out my tape-recorder with a new cassette, the front doors of the hotel swung open, an entourage of representatives from both the "MINREX" (Ministry of External Relations) and the Ministry of Education came into the hall, with one man—tall and gray-haired—leading all the rest.

Several people in the lobby nodded or saluted as the man came straight for me and Martha, seated in our chairs.

Martha looked alarmed—an unusual reaction. She was almost always self-possessed.

I asked: "Who is he?"

But there was no time for a reply. He was standing right before us now.

I rose from my chair. He offered his hand, gave me a solid handshake, then announced in a surprisingly soft voice: "There are certain schools you ought to get a chance to see. I've thought of three or four that are within a five-hour drive. How do you feel?"

I said that I felt fine.

"Come on. Let's go!" he said. "I want to get there while the pupils are in class." And, as the visitors and desk-clerks stood about and stared, he took us by the arms and swept us through the lobby and right out the door. An Alfa Romeo van was waiting at the steps, its sliding panel open. The representatives of the Ministry of Education and the MINREX were already seated quietly inside.

I took the seat behind the driver; Martha took the seat closest behind me, for easiest translation, and my new (and still mysterious) friend pulled out the drop-seat on my side. The motor purred. The driver shifted into gear. The gold-and-purple van roared off from the hotel.

"I would like to introduce myself," he finally announced. "I hope you will forgive me for not doing so before, but I was eager to get out of the hotel. I am José Ramón Fernández. It is my obligation both to govern and to supervise all levels of the Cuban public schools."

Still, I must have looked surprised. He added, therefore, in a slightly hoarse but gentle voice, "I am the Education Minister of Cuba."

At last I started to get hold of the idea that the whirlwind visit which I was about to make into the Cuban public schools would take place in the company of the man who had the job of making sure that every need and possible precondition for the operation of these schools had been fulfilled. I was, in short, with one of the three or four true leaders of the Cuban revolution.

The car was equipped with complex communication apparatus. The driver moved at a speed that kept me in a state of marginal uneasiness almost the whole time. Nobody else, except for Martha (who was frightened by all high-speed driving), seemed to notice that the needle on the dashboard read above one hundred kilometers per hour almost the full duration of the ride.

Martha now began what she reported, later on, to have been the most demanding five hours of her entire career. Her gift for simultaneous translation is so good that very soon I ceased to recognize her role at all and, for long periods of time, forgot her presence or her mediation. It was only when the tour was over and I saw her sitting in complete exhaustion in that small seat behind me, on the ride back to the hotel, that I suddenly recognized that all I had heard, and almost all that I had learned that day, had been translated by her skill and perseverance.

Fernández started off by opening up a map and giving me a rapid-fire overview of new schools-in-the-country in the region of Havana. Green squares were dotted in all sections of the province. Each one represented a new school in operation. Yellow squares (a larger number than the green) represented those that would be finished and in operation, as he hoped, by 1980.

"I'd like to pick three schools at random. They don't know that we are coming. If they do, it changes things. We'll take the risk . . ."

Folding the map, he launched into an energetic monologue:

"In Cuba the infant death-rate is now twenty-three per thousand. You can compare this for yourself with other Third World nations and with Western European nations, too. We had six thousand doctors here in Cuba, prior to the triumph of the revolution. Most of them practiced only in the richest sections of the major cities. Half of them left for Florida once General Batista fled. Today we have eleven thousand M.D.'s—one physician to nine hundred people.

"We place much emphasis on rural polyclinics, on infant health, and on prenatal care. In Cuba the store-windows may not seem to be so full as in Chicago, or Caracas or San Juan, but there are no children hungry, no children sick without physicians present, nor are there schoolchildren without schools. We think of these things, as you must understand, whenever the U.S. press speaks of the scarcity of luxuries in Cuba . . ."

Arrowing in more closely on the public schools, Fernández rattled off a number of statistics—some of which I had already heard: "In twenty months, following the triumph of the revolution, ten thousand new schools were established—large numbers being former military barracks. After the revolution had been in power for a total of two years, we had doubled the number of pupils from first grade through senior high. We now have 1,900,000 children in elementary school, 700,000 in the junior high and high schools, 632,000 adults in a number of extension schools, night schools and such, 125,000 university pupils, 36,000 teachers being graduated from the pedagogic institutes each year.

"In 1958, under Batista, the government invested less than eighty million pesos in the education of the people. My budget for 1976 is nine hundred and sixty million pesos. This is the largest single budget out of all the ministries."

I asked Fernández if he was including military costs in this statement. He answered that he was. "I do not have at hand the military budget for the present year, but I can tell you that the education budget is by far the largest. We spend over one hundred pesos for each citizen of Cuba. If we consider only those who are involved in education, the per-pupil average is approximately three times larger. In your terms, at the present rate of exchange, it would be about three hundred fifty dollars.

"Our goal is that all citizens who are fifteen years or older will have attained the ninth-grade level in the next few years. The conditions needed to achieve this goal have, by now, in large part, been created. Two hundred sixty thousand workers are devoted wholly to some portion of the pedagogic task. This represents approximately eight to ten percent of our entire work-force. Of these, one hundred fifty thousand are the classroom teachers. The rest are cooks, technicians, nurses, subdirectors, and the like.

"The school that we are going to visit first is one of four hundred now in full-scale operation: thirty-eight teachers and six hundred pupils . . . twenty-eight hours of class per week, ten hours of quiet study, three of sports, two of art instruction, fifteen hours to work out in the fields . . . Each school costs one million pesos for construction—three hundred sixty thousand for all costs of operation in one year . . ."

I looked at Martha. She was already wilting in the heat of the mid-morning, but, closing her eyes, as she had once explained it, "to assist my concentration," she kept right on at an uninterrupted pace.

"Work, in our belief, is a necessity for man. Intellectual, scientific, research, or whatever—but it must be useful work. If not, a person lives a parasitic life upon the social order. A man or woman who does not work has got to understand that somebody else has been obliged to do the work which he has left undone. In Cuba we lack oil, we lack diamonds, we lack gold. Our major resource is the land. That is one reason why our emphasis in education has been turned in this direction."

The minister, at my request, spoke next about the

origin of the concept: "schools *en campo.*" The idea had begun ten years before with an experiment in rural living, a plan that was devised to send as many boys and girls of junior high school age as possible to spend a period of forty-five days in the country as a normal portion of their school year. The initial idea ("schools-*to*-the country") was for studies to continue while the students did productive labor at the side of campesinos who would share with them their knowledge of the soil, of the land, the crops, the care of cattle, and the like.

Although one obvious goal for all of this was the productive power of young people, there was also a concomitant political/psychological intention: Cuban educators wanted to devise a means by which young people might grow up to view themselves not as consumers of things made by others, but rather as producers of things that other people *need.*

One hundred forty thousand pupils were involved in the first year of schools-to-the-country, not in the form of organized brigades, but rather as the student bodies of entire schools. In the second year, the number of participants expanded to one hundred sixty thousand. Teachers, however, complained that students could not do a full day of productive labor and sustain the burden of their studies at the same time. A reduction, therefore, in both work and academic pressure became a guideline for the program's second year.

One year later, in spite of modifications, it became apparent that schools-to-the-country were not working out. The forty-five days removed from class proved to be an interruption in the academic year that could not be made up. Moreover, the days in the country and those in the city were not integrated in a way by which the one might give some resonance and practical value to the other. Instead, the first became a mere diversion from the second.

Finally, the forty-five days out in the country did not give the students adequate time to gain the skills to do a useful job—but proved barely sufficient to provide a minimal adaptation to the work.

Most nations would, by this point, have decided that the whole idea—no matter how well executed—was a theoretical mistake and retreated politely to "the way things were before." Instead, with much the same bravado that had characterized the work of 1961, the government turned the concept of *"al campo"* to *"en campo."* If a forty-five-day visit was a technical mistake, then the obvious solution was to move the whole school to the country: i.e., to build the future junior high schools of the Cuban nation in the countryside right from the start.

"In this way," as Fernández carefully explained, "work and study could be constantly combined; productive labor might attain significant levels, since there would no longer be a self-repeating need to learn the ropes, and study could be closely tied to useful labor on a basis that respected the realistic limits on the strength and energy of teen-age kids."

"The first school-in-the-country was dedicated in June of 1970. By June 1974 one hundred fifty similar schools, each with a capacity of at least five hundred pupils, had been built.

"Today, in 1976, as I have said, the figure for such schools is well above four hundred. By 1980 it is hoped that almost half the junior high school pupils will attend schools-in-the-country. The junior high school population, by that time, will have exceeded the one million mark."

Fernández explained that the buildings are constructed by a rapid and economical method called "Girón"—a prefab system that involves on-site assembly of huge concrete slabs, most of them pure white with brilliant red, green and purple lines and circles, arrows, decorations, banners, exhortations of all kinds.

The schools I saw were airy, open, cheerful, with a lot of breezeways, balconies, and wooden slats in place of glass. Most of them were well equipped with laboratories, meeting centers, libraries, infirmaries, movie theaters, swimming pools, impressive-looking dormitories for the girls and boys—even barbershops and beauty parlors. Students live at school from Sunday evening to midday on Saturday. A mini-bus, assembled in Cuba, offers transportation for all students to their homes on Saturday—and back to school again on Sunday night.

I asked Fernández if he would be willing to reply to criticisms of the whole idea of use of child labor in the fields.

"Our nation," he began, "starts out from a basis of extremely scarce funds, limited teachers, and a limited number of supplies. We are extremely honest with the children on this point. In order to build a beautiful new school, with excellent teachers, new equipment, nurses, libraries, and all, we have to figure out a way to make the school, in some sense, self-sufficient. We cannot afford to build this kind of school, provide good food and health care, books and clothing, transportation, all for free, unless the student body can participate somehow in the process of refinancing its own existence.

"Each school-in-the-country, therefore, is responsible for twelve hundred fifty acres of productive land. This many acres, in the course of three years, produce enough in terms of market worth to underwrite the cost both of construction of the school itself and of its operation. The produce of twelve hundred fifty acres, for example, given over to the cultivation of a citrus fruit should in the course of time be equal to two million pesos every year. One thousand of such schools—which is the goal we have in mind—will not only fully reim-

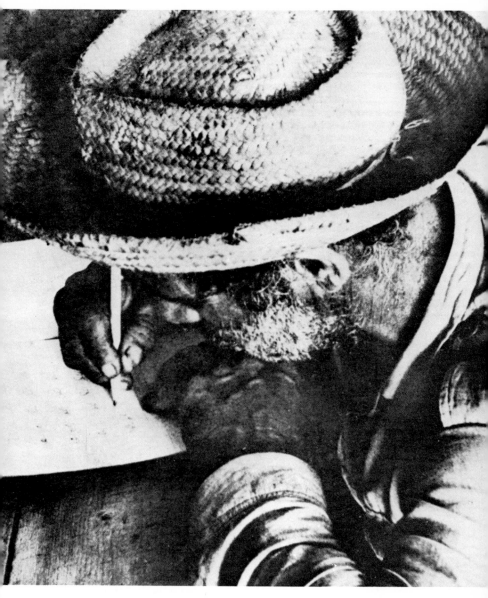

Many of the "teachers" were no more than ten years old,
but thousands of their students were already over sixty-five.

Although the emphasis had been on reading,
mathematics was included, too. . . .

A modified version of the Coleman lantern was produced, first to find one's way from town to town, then to offer light by which to teach and learn (100,000 were produced in 1961).

Student brigadistas were advised to win the loyalty of peasants by working at their sides in the fields.

Habana junio 7 de 1961

Dr Fidel Castro
Ciudad
Compañero Fidel:
Mis deseos son se encuentre bien,
Compañero Fidel Castro
me siento muy contento
apuendi a leer y escribir para defenderme mejor,
grasias a la revolución
Sosialista de los humildes puedo decir.
Patria o Muerte
¡Venceremos!
Año de la Educación.
Ricardo Perez

The final examination was a letter to Fidel. The purpose was to tell him:
"I can *write* and I can *read.*"

The verb form changed once victory was won. *"Venceremos"* turned into
"Vencimos"—"We have overcome!"

Martha Acosta, painstaking translator, loyal friend.
(L. Shumaker)

Juan de la Cruz, curator of the Literacy Museum.
(L. Shumaker)

Photographs in the Literacy Museum:
Manuel Ascunce Domenesch and Conrado Benítez,
two young martyred volunteers.

Maria, a former brigadista,
talking of her part in the Great Campaign.

Christina, telling how she learned to read and write in 1961.
(L. Shumaker)

Christina's teacher, describing her use of the primer *Venceremos*.
(L. Shumaker)

Dr. Raúl Ferrer, one of the leading spirits of the Great Campaign. (L. Shumaker)

Today, Dr. Ferrer is the director of all adult education. (L. Shumaker)

English teacher
and principal of
Che Guevara School.
(L. Shumaker)

A little clowning for the camera. (L. Shumaker)

Participating in an English class at Che Guevara School.

Carlos (second from right) and Jonathan discuss politics. (L. Shumaker)

The principal of the
Martyrs of Kent School.

Students at Martyrs of Kent on the way to the fields.

Girls' dormitory at Martyrs of Kent School.

Between classes at Martyrs of Kent School.

Marisela, Emilia, Barbara, Sandra, Mario:
my team at Martyrs of Kent.

The team goes into a huddle.

A private session with another group at Martyrs of Kent School.

On the way back to school after a work period.

Elementary school children also participate in the fields
for short periods of time.

Secondary pupils concentrate on pure and applied science
at the Lenin School, outside Havana.

burse the costs of education and construction, but will in time begin to make a serious contribution to the value of the Cuban export crop.

"I know that there are those who wish to see the worst in everything we do or say. In this situation, I believe that they will find that they are wasting their own time . . ."

III

The car came to a halt before a bright white concrete structure. I followed Fernández as he stepped from the van, paced carefully across a line of concrete slabs laid out within a handsome decorative pool, marched up the stairs, asked for the headmistress, was told that she was getting ready to be married the next day, but still inquired if she would be willing to come out and say hello.

She soon emerged in plastic curlers, looking dreadfully embarrassed. Fernández, however, seemed to know her well. He introduced her to Martha and me, chatted with her a bit about her personal plans, wished her good luck, then asked:

"Am I invited to the party?"

"I didn't think that you would have the time to come," she said.

"Where is the wedding?" he persisted.

She wrote for him the house, address, and time.

We moved into the breezeway of the school . . .

Fernández kept on giving explanations and projections as we moved: "This kind of school—a boarding school, of course—costs about three times as much per pupil as the day-schools in the city. Nonetheless, as we have seen, the schools pay for themselves in time and manage to serve certain higher goals as well. This school is cheerful, clean, and wholesome. I don't like so much the first ones that we built: plain concrete walls without these decorations, without a swimming pool, or flowerbeds, or these bright-colored halls. This is our goal for secondary schools in Cuba. It is not easy labor for the kids—but we have taken care to be quite sure it is not harmful to their health."

He halted a group of students who were pulling on long rubber boots to head off for the fields. A bit like a reporter with the speech-rate of an anti-aircraft battery, he asked them various questions that concerned their work:

"What are you growing? How many hours do you work? Is the work too hard? Do you have the time to study? How is your food? Are the teachers okay? Do they prepare their lessons well—so that you can truly understand? Why are you going out so late? Isn't the work supposed to start a little earlier than ten A.M.? Where are the other members of this group—of this brigade? Why aren't your teachers with you? Are they waiting in the field? What do you study? How many hours of class lessons? How many hours to do homework? Do you think it was a good idea to come here? Should we build a lot more schools like these? How many want to live out in the country later on?"

The kids, who seemed to know him, gave him rapid-fire answers. Many had broad smiles on their faces as he spoke. No one looked scared. A number seemed amused.

Back in the car Fernández went right on: "There is a nurse in every school. The productivity rate of pupils is said by some to be one half that of adults. I believe that one third is a more precise and careful figure. There are certain areas that are far too difficult for children of this age. Sugarcane, for instance—it is, honestly, back-breaking work. On the other hand, there are certain areas—tobacco, coffee beans, small berries—where the children can do better work than adult campesinos, mainly because their hands are soft and gentle and do not destroy so large a portion of the crop in harvest season."

Without transition Fernández turned his thoughts to an entirely different theme: "All of our schools, of course, do not restrict themselves to agricultural labor of this kind. There are also schools that place their emphasis on animal breeding, cattle farming, eggs and poultry, and the like. If you will accept my own suggestion, I hope you will later pay a visit to one of the dairy schools." He spoke for a time about the need for work in animal genetics and went into considerable detail in regard to various breeds. "If you visit one of the new breeding centers, it may be that you will wonder if the purpose of the center is to breed the kind of cattle that will yield more meat, or whether the goal is for a greater milk production. The meat is less important than the milk. Cuba does not need to raise a vast amount of beef. We must become a nation that lives more upon the fish and other seafoods from the ocean on all sides. It is milk that matters to us most."

We pulled up at a second school. This time, not even stopping to address the school's director, Fernández walked right through the breezeway to confront a group of kids who were returning from the fields—unlike the previous group, whom we had met on their way *out.*

Again he fired questions at the kids. There was humor in his manner and a lot of reaching out of hands, affectionate tousling of the hair, joking, teasing—and a look of mischief in his eyes.

"What did you do? Did you pick berries? What kind? Strawberries? Do you think that you will give us a good crop? How do you feel? Are you all tired out? You must be the teacher. Am I correct? You look worn out. I think you weigh a bit too much. It doesn't set a good example for the boys and girls. Do you think that you could lose a few more pounds? Twenty pounds, perhaps, in twenty days? Don't mind my teasing you! I see that you are doing a good job . . ."

This time, to my satisfaction, we had a chance to visit a class that was just winding up its final lessons before lunch. It was a ninth-grade English class. Fernández introduced me as a *"reportero norteamericano."*

The room was silent only for a moment. Then one boy asked without the slightest hesitation, even in the presence of Fernández: "Not another *asesino?*"

The girl sitting beside him clapped her hand over her mouth.

I said to him that I was not a murderer. I said I was a *"yanqui,"* but that I was not "an *asesino,"* nor a *"gringo"*—and "I am not Nelson Rockefeller, either."

Most of the children in the class began to smile.

I asked the students what they thought about the U.S.A. One student said: "We like the people who come here to visit as our friends from the United States. We do not believe the people of the U.S. are the same thing as the government of the United States."

I said that I agreed with him completely on that point. I also told him that I felt a sense of gratitude to be among young people who could be so patient on a subject which must be so painful in the wake of many recent provocations.

"No," said the classroom teacher. "We do not think that this is something special. We think it is entirely normal that we ought to feel a sense of kinship with the people of the U.S.A."

After a pause: "We have a common enemy, after all."

I puzzled for a minute—and then asked him whom he had in mind.

"The CIA," was his reply.

The class broke into laughter—carefully, however, lest the joke be too much at my expense.

Fernández asked me if I had some final question for the students. I told him simply that I felt great admiration for the hard work and persistence of the pupils in sustaining an important role in Cuba's economic life. The children stood beside their desks and waved to us as we went out the door.

In the car once more, during a relatively short hop, Fernández plowed right on with his statistics, guidelines, and beliefs.

"In each school you will find that half the pupils will be members of the UJC [Young Communist League]. The work process is especially important to us when the pupils recognize a clear, direct, and human value in the labor that they do. It is important that they understand that oranges do not come from plastic packages in the store, but that an orange is the fruit of human toil. This is the special sense in which we use the phrase 'productive' labor . . .

"The oranges grown by many of the children in this school that we just saw will be provided to the younger brothers, sisters, cousins, of these children. Others will be pulverized for concentrated juice. The seeds are used to feed the animals. The peel and the rind are used for marmalade. Before long, citrus will become a major portion of our export trade . . ."

The third school at which we stopped was getting set for lunch as we arrived. Fernández marched straight down the hall into the dining room, asked several pupils if the food was good, got a mixed bag of approving and complaining answers, and proceeded, therefore, with more than a touch of irritation, through the kitchen doors.

He demanded to be told what was being served for lunch that day. (It was apparent that he was no stranger to the children or the adults of this school.) After each item, he would ask: "What else?" When he came to a huge vat of soup he asked what it was made from and then grabbed a giant ladle and began to stir the soup in order to see if it contained significant amounts of meat or fish.

He rolled the substance slowly over the spoon's edge and seemed to make a mental note to deal with this at some point soon. He was more happy with the menu for dinner, already in preparation in another section of the kitchen. The main course was being made from thousands of ground-up sardines. The salad looked fresh. There were boiled potatoes, ice cream for dessert—a good meal for six hundred kids.

We left the school by a back exit, and because it was already after one o'clock, Fernández asked his driver to pick up a little speed. Martha looked alarmed but never slowed down the pace of her translation.

"What have we seen? What is the sum total of it all? First, I think you need to understand that even though these schools have been expanded to accommodate six hundred pupils, rather than five hundred as we first had planned, there have been no cutbacks in the services provided—nor in our pedagogic expectations from each school.

"Second, I want to be quite sure that you have recognized the three essential purposes of schools like these. We would not settle on a course of secondary education that was so expensive and demanding if we did not feel that there were powerful reasons for a sweeping transformation of this kind. The first goal, of course, is to enable pupils to assist their government in building up an economic base. The produce of these schools, as I have said, will have to reimburse us for the cost of operation and construction.

"A more important goal is to enable these young people to develop an undying sense of reverence for productive labor of a manual nature. We do not know how many of these children will decide to come back to the rural areas, after these three years are done, in order to do animal husbandry, or citrus farming, or whatnot. Some of them will—and those who do, of course, will have had superb experience. They will be technologically expert in agricultural production. They will also be profoundly cultured human beings.

"Neither of these, however, is the final goal, and neither would have given us sufficient reason to create schools-in-the-country as a national objective, if there were not something more. In the long run, whether or not these kids come back someday to lead this kind of life, they will not forget the sense of working with their hands beside the campesinos.

"One of the tragedies of our nation for one hundred and fifty years has been the separation of the urban population from the land. We believe that it is not just basic to survival as a nation, but basic to our moral unity as well, that we be able to achieve a reconciliation. José Martí annunciated the ideal in 1883. I am sure that you have heard it many times by now. It is a crime to separate the people from the land. The goal of the schools you have been visiting today is to erase that evil heritage forever."

Before we were done, I asked Fernández if he would tell me something of his childhood, his education, and his life before the revolution.

"I was born to a middle-class family," he replied. "I was a religious child. My convictions as a Christian were destroyed at age eleven when I entered a religious school. I later went to a cadet school and was trained to be an expert in the military arts. I specialized in artillery and completed my preparation in November 1952. Soon after, I became instructor in a military school. Meanwhile, I joined a number of others in a plot to overthrow Batista. I was discovered and convicted and was sent to the Isle of Pines. I was arrested in April 1956 and released the first of January, 1959.

"I was not a Marxist prior to the time of my arrest, but I had already a strong sense of the intolerable side of Cuban life: the hunger and the misery of the poor. When we tried to overthrow Batista in the army, we did not think about Marxism. We only thought of ending the corruption and deceit. When I went to jail, I had the time and opportunity at last to read a lot of things I'd never known. I read, for the first time, about Marxism. I also met a number of profound and dedicated Marxists who became my friends . . .

"How is it, then, that Fidel came to be aware of me? I had had no real connection with the group that planned Moncada. Nonetheless, in prison there were many members of that group. I was not a member of M-26 ['Movement of the Twenty-Sixth of July'], but I was elected chairman of the prisoners' committee. Another prisoner with me in that period was Armando Hart. Fidel selected him a little later as his minister of education.

"After the revolution I became director of an officer-training school not far from here, in the province of Matanzas. I was there in 1961. It was a school, not a combat unit, but I was the closest of the military leaders to the place your government still calls the Bay of Pigs. I received a call by telephone at two or three A.M. and was given command of our defense by order of Fidel.

145

We assembled our forces in a sugar mill close by. We were at Girón by nine A.M. Overflights and random bombing had been taking place since dawn: C-47's, disguised as Cuban planes . . . The B-26, I think, was also used. In all I believe that fifteen were shot down. When the paratroopers started coming down around eleven, we were prepared to give them a good welcome."

I asked Fernández whether it was true that Cuban exile forces had attacked civilian targets such as hospitals and schools.

"No, I do not think they purposely attacked these targets," he replied. "It was not intentional—but it was indiscriminate."

In a quiet voice Fernández said: "I still retain a high opinion of the U.S. population, as you know. It is the use to which your government has dedicated both its money and its power I condemn. I had always believed, and still believe today, that Adlai Stevenson was totally deceived about the role of the U.S. by his own leaders. He was an honest man whom many of us liked. It is my own belief that this destroyed him . . ."

Fernández had fallen into a somber and reflective state of mind. "Well, all of that, of course, is in the past. It is a long way back and we are living for another generation now . . ."

Fernández was late for a two o'clock appointment. He asked his driver to turn off onto a new, as-yet-unopened superhighway. Speeding along at more than one hundred kilometers per hour, he continued chatting with me in his quiet, confident voice—until we suddenly found ourselves heading straight into a phalanx of six Soviet tanks, the only military hardware I had ever seen close up in Cuba. Right behind the tanks was a line of antiaircraft rocket launchers and, behind those, another row of tanks. Fernández quickly pointed to my tape-recorder, which I instantly turned off. The driver went right up on the embankment while the tanks and rocket launchers thundered by.

As we descended, to continue on our way, Fernández made one brief remark. "That," he said, "is very important, too. Nobody will ever again be able to drop bombs on one of the schools that we have seen today and leave this land alive." After that, without a pause, he was back again discussing education.

"All education has forever a class bias. No society will foster schools that do not serve its ends. Education is not merely technical instruction, nor the passing-on of information. It is the total training of the human character—its essence and its soul. In the period of Watergate I used to ask: What is the ethical preparation that these men were given in *their* public schools?"

These proved to be almost his final words to me that day. We had arrived at last at my hotel. I could not help but make one observation in the course of telling him goodbye. I said that something in his manner and his style made me think, for a reason that I could not say, of certain North American leaders I had known. Something about his manner struck me as familiar.

He laughed outright, placed his hands upon my shoulder, looked briefly at his colleagues, and then said to me, in perfect English: "It is not a great surprise. I received part of my education, thanks to the kindness of the North American people, in a U.S. military school. I spent a good while in your nation, and I traveled about during my vacations in an old used Chevrolet. Some of us went together to New Orleans for the Mardi Gras. We made a number of good friends. That, of course, was long before the overthrow of the dictator . . ."

A firm handshake and the day was done. Martha and I retired for a cold beer to the dark and air-conditioned bar of the hotel.

The next day, a little before sunset, I was walking by the sea near my hotel. A group of four boys had gathered just ahead of me, beside the Malecón. As I walked along the group came closer. They greeted me in English, as if we were old friends.

"How did you like our school?" one student said.

I asked him, "Did I meet you?"

"Yes," he said. "You were visiting on Friday noon with Minister Fernández. You came into my class. We joked a lot when you were there—and then we talked about the CIA."

I remembered the classroom now, and so—instead of giving them a simple and polite reply—I took the opportunity to ask a question that had been within my mind. "If this is so, then let me ask you one more question that has bothered me a bit. How does it turn out that you happen to know the minister so well? Is it from seeing him so often on TV?"

The boy replied: "Everybody in our classroom knows Fernández. He visits with us a lot of times—sometimes with friends like you, sometimes alone."

"What do you think of him? Is he a truthful man? Do you believe he visits your school out of real interest? Or do you think that possibly he visits you so that you will be prepared to make a good impression on a visiting reporter like myself? Why else would he come and visit you so much? He must know lots of other schools in Cuba, too."

"He comes into our school *without* reporters," the young man said again. "He visits us a lot of days to learn, to check, just for the fun sometimes. He goes into the fields and works with us as well. He visits us in class and he comes into the dorms to see if everything is clean and healthy, too."

"Then do you think his visits are for real? Or does he

simply know the moment when it is just right for him to put on a good show for someone from the U.S.A.?"

"Nobody in Cuba needs to put on a performance for the U.S.A.," the student said.

We strolled along and talked a little more: four young Cuban kids and I, beside the sea.

"You know you can come back again to visit," I was told by one of the young men. "Even without the minister, you would still be welcome in our school."

Part Four

On My Own

(A Yankee Teacher in the Cuban Schools)

I

In the long run, as every teacher knows, there is only one way to find out what is really going on within a school.

It is to go to the school and to find out on your own, without the experts, without the minister who is also a hero and a former *comandante*, without the municipal supervisor and, if it is polite and possible, without the school director. It is to go to the children, to go into their dorms, into their classrooms and (if they will allow you there) into their trust and confidence as well.

On my own, as a final check to all that had been said, and even all that I had seen while in the company of various leaders of the Cuban schools, I went back to Cuba one year later, in the fall of 1977, in order to visit a number of secondary schools, to do so with minimal supervision and with a good deal less reliance on the help of a translator.

I also spent my weekends and most evenings on my own, hopping buses and walking a great deal so that I would have a chance to see all corners of Havana—not just the beautiful high-rise complex built in Alemar to house exemplary workers and their kids, but also the subdivided nineteen-twenties houses, now broken into two or three apartments, as well as some of the poorer corrugated-metal-covered houses of small farmers in the rural sections on the edge of town.

My bus- and walking-tours brought me into direct dialogue with many Cuban men and women, boys and girls. More than once while I was riding on a bus, a group of kids would crowd around and speak to me, much as they had done the year before. At least three times this happened: Kids whom I had met in passing during a twenty-minute visit to their class would recognize me out in the street, or on a bus, and would engage me in an easy-going chat. It was an excellent chance for me to double-check the claims of higher-ups.

Finally, it seems important to observe that all of the school visits that I made in 1977 were to schools of my own choice. On several occasions as Martha and I passed one school en route to another I had chosen in advance, I would ask if we could stop and make a detour in order to observe a school that would not be expecting guests. In no case was my request refused.

This, then, is the story of the classroom visits that I made throughout Havana Province during 1977—"unprotected"—an American classroom teacher, on my own.

II

The first two schools I chose to visit were selected mainly because of my sentimental fascination with their names. The first of them was intended to be the first of all the schools *en campo*—a model for the rest. It turned out, instead, to be the second. Nonetheless, it has one great distinction: Alone of all the schools *en campo* this one bears the name of Che Guevara.

The school—now in its seventh year—is not so splendid, nor so modernistic, as any of the three schools that I visited with Minister Fernández. It is composed, like all the other junior highs, of three concrete and prefabricated buildings: classrooms, dining area, and student dorms, each connected to the next by an attractive open breezeway. The buildings are surrounded by twelve hundred fifty acres of rich tropical soil, planted primarily with orange trees.

As in all of these schools, the student body is somewhat above five hundred. There are forty-five teachers (including student-teachers) and a vigorous young principal, María Elena, twenty-five years old. She greets me casually, holding out her hand to shake my own, and smiling in an easygoing way.

As in most schools of Cuba, there are photographs of Marx, Martí, Camilo (a brave revolutionary leader who was killed in a plane accident in 1959), Tania (who died in the struggle in Bolivia with Che), Lenin, and Allende, smaller photographs of Fidel—some at the entranceway, some in the corridors or meeting rooms or classrooms. In the office of María Elena, however, there is only one large photo: the same one that I have looked at, on my living-room wall in the United States since 1968. It is the classic picture, white on black, with one star centered at the front of his beret . . .

"We shall be like Che," the children of Cuba chant together, when they walk along, in blue shorts, white shirts, and red berets, as members of the Young Pioneers. Here in this secondary school *en campo*, the slogan takes on a more poignant meaning.

The children and teachers of Comandante Ernesto Che Guevara seem to sense that the name of their school brings with it a unique historic mandate. There is in this school a spirit of collective pride, unusual even in the context of the Cuban revolution. The best evidence of this collective spirit is found, ironically, in the *ages* of the pupils in the school. One recognizes, with sudden surprise, that the kids are far too old to be the pupils of an ordinary junior high, too physically mature to be in lower-level secondary.

My question brings from the principal a self-confident and amusing smile: "It is the truth. This is an unusual school—the only one I know in which this sort of thing has taken place. The student body, at the end of their three years in 1975, voted that they did not want to leave! The school spirit was extremely strong. Nobody wanted to leave their teachers and their friends. So they asked permission (and their teachers joined them) to see if the minister of education would allow them to remain here for the next three years as well: in other words, to turn this school into *pre-universidad*.

"This was their request and they received permission to keep on in the same school, but with a much more difficult curriculum, of course. So they remained, and we became—for now, at least—an upper-secondary school *en campo*. I believe we are the only school exactly like this."

I spend most of my morning at the Che Guevara School with students of the English language and their teacher, Celia Santamaría, a graduate of Havana University.

"Most of our pupils will proceed to universities if they so desire," she reports. "Last year, there was not one pupil who did not go to the university from here."

It is a little odd to hear unhesitant statements of this kind: the sort of thing that one might hear at an exclusive prep school in the U.S. The children, however, are not the children of "particular" families. Admission is by examination only, as well as by assessment of the pupil's character. If two applicants have roughly equal grades, the nod will go to the one who has displayed the greatest willingness to share what he or she has learned with others who are not so highly skilled.

The class, which already reads and writes in English, is about to begin a rapid oral drill. Celia explains to me beforehand that in their written work her pupils are now done with most grammatical instruction and are concentrating mainly on interpretation of diverse materials, ranging from technical books to poetry and fiction. They write essays on their families, school activities, and personal ideas. Some of their essays, I observe, are on political subjects also.

The oral drill seems excellent in terms of pace and

emphasis. It is a fast-moving alternation between the teacher asking questions, the full class giving answers, and the teacher asking individual pupils to speak out. Within a span of only fifteen minutes half the pupils have already spoken on their own, as well as in full group. Not one word of Spanish is pronounced during the class.

The text Celia uses (*Practical English*, Havana, 1972) is badly dated, with its "mother does this, father does that" approach—but soon appears to kids and teachers both to be a well acknowledged joke. Its out-of-date male-female role assignments would be catas-trophic if it were not for the obvious facts (a) that class and teacher *recognize* that it is archaic in its subject-matter, (b) that pupil discussion, as, for instance, in the class on "Political Fundamentals," concentrates repeat-edly on women's rights and on the newly promulgated Family Code, and (c) that the same students will, two hours hence, be working side-by-side, as absolute equals, in the orange groves that stretch out from the school on every side.

This morning's drill from *Practical English* tells us of "the Sawyers," a Canadian family who have come to live and work in Cuba. It is only in this manner that the author of the practice sentences can figure out a way to situate an English-speaking family in a setting that the pupils will find recognizable. (In my own view, isolated readings from Jack London, Ernest Hemingway, or E. B. White would have been a lot more interesting to the class, even if the setting had to be in San Francisco or New York.)

The practice text, in any event, proves to be a fascinat-ing hybrid of two nationalities, two world-views, and two worlds:

"We are speaking about Mr. Sawyer."

"Does Mr. Sawyer go to work in the morning or in the afternoon?"

"Are the Sawyers Canadian or Cuban?"

"What are the Sawyers doing here in Cuba?"

"The Sawyers have come to help as teachers in the revolution . . ."

"Does Mrs. Sawyer help in CDR activities or in the FMC?"

The teacher asks fifteen questions and receives fast answers, picking up on small pronunciation errors, requesting second, third, and fourth attempts to get things right. She seems meticulous in noticing even the smallest deviations—so much so that I start to cringe when she comes down the aisle near the seat I've been assigned.

Towards the end of the text there is a bit of dialogue about the weekend: "Is it nice to have our breakfast in the morning?"

"Yes, it is nice to have our breakfast in the morning. But it is even nicer to sleep late!"

The class laughs and the period is over. The method is conventional—the subject-matter square, traditional, absurd; but the mood of the class is comfortable and the teacher's personal friendliness with the pupils is apparent. Two hours later she will be working in the hot sun with some of the same group, plucking newly ripened oranges from the trees.

As the class comes to an end, one of the pupils asks if he can talk with me, along with several of the other pupils, on a balcony outside. He says he likes to talk with visitors from Canada and from the U.S., in order to help him with pronunciation. The group, young men and women both, join me in a little circle on a shaded balcony. I ask Martha to stay with us, in order to bridge the language gap in case the words and phrases come to be too esoteric or complex. The teacher, however, stays at a distance—in recognition of my stated wish to be alone with pupils for whatever periods of time I choose.

The student who first approached me asks my name —and then tells me his own: "My name is Carlos." If it is his desire to polish his pronunciation, it is mine to find out how he feels about some of the issues in the news today. I ask him first about the issue of the rights of women. I am given a quick response not from Carlos, but from a young woman who appears about sixteen.

"Women still have struggles ahead but we are far closer to being equal now in Cuba than at any time before. We are *not* like 'Mrs. Sawyer,' if you had that in your mind!"

Her own amusement and the laughter in the group reinforce my faith that even a ludicrous and outdated text cannot undercut the larger lesson of a lived equality within the school itself.

I ask the group another question that is on my mind: "What about prisons? What is the purpose of imprisonment—or execution? Do you think that people should be put in prison for the 'wrong' beliefs or only for a criminal deed?"

Carlos replies in careful sentences of measured thought and of meticulous pronunciation: "First of all, so far as I know, execution does not still exist in Cuba. If it does, I am against it. I consider it a great mistake. I do not believe in capital punishment. I also do not think that people in our nation are arrested for the 'wrong beliefs.' If it is only a matter of belief, then we can help those people in our schools, or in the CDR, or in the working center . . ."

I try to force the issue: "Are you quite sure of what you have just said? I am of the general belief that more than one man or woman lives in prison here within your nation, not for his or her 'bad deeds,' but rather for political opinion."

160

He looks me in the eyes and he replies: *"It is not so.* It would not be in keeping with the character of Fidel and with the views that he upholds. If it is true, I am not afraid to tell you that it is a fact for which I feel great shame. I will find out."

He adds these words: "It may be that what your government leaders call 'political prisoners' in *our* situation might turn out to be the people they would call 'war criminals' in *theirs*. I mean, by this, that—to my knowledge—there have been people who have tried to damage harvests, which would mean the hunger of our people, and others who have tried to blow up buildings, bridges, military targets, and—perhaps on purpose or possibly by chance—have dropped their bombs or fired their weapons on civilian targets, too. People have died. Animals that we have counted upon to feed our children have been poisoned with infection. Maybe you have heard of the swine flu.

"Is it possible that the reporters of the U.S.A. would use a different standard in our own case than in yours? If these people are in prison for their viewpoints, then I believe this is a serious mistake; but, if they are in prison for their criminal behavior, then I believe they should remain in prison, maybe for ten or maybe twenty years. That is about the length of time that it would take to heal a person of the wish to do these kinds of things..."

It does not seem fair to press the issue any further. I am convinced that this young man will not relent until he knows the truth (or feels he knows the truth) for sure.

I try to shift the conversation to a slightly different issue: "Do you really think that prisons ever make a worthwhile transformation in the character or in the behavior of a human being?"

"If prisons are good, I think that they can change the tendencies—the inclinations—of a human being, such as the case of a person who would sell narcotics to school children. When prisoners learn their lessons, when we find the way to *teach* them to learn something new, then I think they should be free."

I ask Carlos if he also feels that this is the government's point of view.

"I do not know, so I should not reply. But I have told you what I personally believe."

"Do you think there is a time when prisons will no longer be required in the world—when people will no longer need to be locked up behind steel bars?"

His answer to this question is the one, of all those I have heard today, which I will not forget. "When Cuba reaches the communist stage," he says, "we will have no problems about theft and murder."

I ask him, "Isn't Cuba communist *today?*"

"We are not yet at a communist stage," he answers, in that same earnest and explanatory voice that he has used in speaking to me all along. "We are still a socialist society. When all of the world is communist, then we will all be like one family. All of the nations will work for everyone to help each other. There will be no murder, sabotage, or counter-revolution."

"Until that time will you need prisons?"

"Yes. Until then it will be essential," he replies.

The teacher calls to Carlos and the rest to warn them that they'll miss their lunch if they don't get it now. Each student shakes my hand and says "goodbye" or else "good luck." Carlos, however, waits to say his own goodbye. His final words come out a bit mixed up: "I am very glad to see you visit here. I also hope that you will come to visit once again . . . Send my regards!"

An hour later, when we leave the school, they wave to me and shout some more "goodbyes," as our driver passes just beside them, in their work-clothes, on their way out to the fields.

III

In leaving the Ernesto Che Guevara School, I have the sense of having learned a great deal more than what I bargained for. Nonetheless, it is the visit of the following day that looms the largest in my mind. This is the single visit, of all visits I have made in Cuba, that I value most. Many days within the Cuban schools are special for one reason or another; but this is a day that I have thought about, have hoped for, and anticipated now for almost a full year.

The soil this morning, as we head out to the country once again, is rich-looking and very, very red. The sugarcane rises high above our heads on either side. We approach the school through a neighborhood of flat fields, interrupted by occasional hills or buttes—cut off abruptly at times, as if by sand-excavation. Orchards, cornfields, citrus groves, and palm trees are on both sides of the road. Many small houses have in their front yard a single cow.

The driver of our car navigates rapidly past the

thatch-roof houses of the campesinos, slows down for a horse-drawn wagon, slows down twice again as we pass in and out of two small towns. At last, after about one hour's drive directly west out of Havana, he comes to a halt as we approach the gateway to a school, then turns a sharp left, and goes speeding up the drive.

The school is slightly older than the one we visited the day before. This was the first of all the schools *en campo* to be built, furnished, supplied with books, provided with its staff and pupils, and then dedicated by Fidel. Initially, it was expected that this one, *being* the first, would bear the name of Che. The date, however, was June of 1970 and news of the protests in the colleges and universities of the United States had been disseminated widely by the Cuban press. At the last moment, at the request of pupils, faculty and staff, Fidel agreed to change the name of the first new school *en campo* as a symbol of respect for those in the United States who had been working to attempt to stop the war in Vietnam. The school for this reason stands today beneath the name selected by its first five hundred pupils: School of the Martyrs of Kent.

Much like the Che Guevara School, but unlike those brand-new schools that I had seen with Minister Fernández, Martyrs of Kent is not a showpiece of red, blue, and purple circles, stripes, slogans, and banners. It lacks a beautiful flowerbed, a decorative pool before its doorway, an Olympic pool for kids and teachers to enjoy an evening swim. Its concrete slabs are of a pink-grey color. Its windows are thin wooden slats tinted blue. In four directions from the central complex, fields of beets and sugarcane—and large, long stretches of banana trees—extend out to the point at which the land lifts softly and then falls.

If the school is lacking in the lavish decorations of the newest of the new schools-in-the-country, Martyrs of

Kent has a meaning for the pupils of this school, and for the people of this nation, which no other school could possibly convey. Many schools in Cuba bear the names of those who have been dead for fifty or one hundred years. This one alone exists to honor those who were almost contemporaries of the children who now study in its classrooms and who walk within its halls. I do not know if there is even one school in all of the United States that pays this simple tribute to those four young people.

I start by visiting classrooms chosen, by my custom, without warning. One is a physics class. A strict young man is talking about levers. There is a formula on the blackboard that I cannot understand. On the back wall there is a poster bearing all the marks of student impulse, anger, indignation: "Against The Neutron Bomb!" There is another, left there undoubtedly from the spring before: "Seventh Anniversary, May 4, 1970."

In an exuberant English class, conducted by an energetic and engaging teacher, a pleasant breeze blows through the open wood slats—and the English conversation is nonstop. Teachers and students toss the dialogue back and forth as if it were a volleyball:

"Mary is a student."

"Miriam is an engineer."

"Paul is a teacher."

"Peter is an actor."

"Is Miriam an actress?"

"No! Miriam is an engineer!"

When a student speaks with insufficient clarity, the teacher races forward to inquire: "Pardon me?"

A student who gets the words all wrong receives an English schoolmarm's teasing: "Oh! No, no, my dear!"

When the teacher wants full-class participation, she invites the pupils with a pleasant phrase: "Let's go!"

The answer from one of the students isn't quite right

165

or quite wrong. She makes an amusing puzzled face and says: "So-so!"

At last the students start to get in the momentum of the lesson. "Very good! Keep on! Let's go!"

A wonderful, animated teacher, but I have encountered other lively teachers many times in other Cuban schools. This is the school named for the four who were shot down at Kent State. Their faces line the walls as one walks into the first breezeway of the school. Something here has got to be unique . . .

I go in to see the well-stocked library. Once again I am predictably impressed. I scribble titles:

War and Peace, Tolstoi (15 copies); *Fathers and Sons,* Turgenyev (15 copies); *Three Musketeers,* Dumas (18 copies); *An American Tragedy,* Dreiser (17 copies); *The Story of My Life,* Charles Chaplin (7 copies); *Claude Debussy: Biography* (10 copies); *Friedrich Engels: Biography* (10 copies); *Twenty Thousand Leagues Under the Sea,* Jules Verne (12 copies); *Tom Sawyer,* Mark Twain (20 copies); *Swiss Family Robinson,* Wyss (10 copies); *Just So!,* Kipling (15 copies); *Journey of a Naturalist,* Darwin (15 copies); *Shorter Writings of Karl Marx* (15 copies); *Ten Days That Shook the World,* John Reed (7 copies); *David Copperfield,* Charles Dickens (20 copies); *Oliver Twist,* Charles Dickens (20 copies); *Selected Works,* Euripides, Homer, Aristophanes (10 copies each); *Man's Fate,* Malraux (15 copies); *The Red and the Black,* Stendhal (20 copies); *Sorrows of Young Werther,* Goethe (15 copies); *Tales of Hoffmann, an Anthology* (10 copies); *Buddenbrooks,* Thomas Mann (10 copies); *Selected Works,* Edgar Allan Poe (10 copies); *In the Struggle,* La Pasionaria (15 copies) . . .

It is a good, diverse collection; but this too is not unique: not very different from a dozen other libraries in which I poke around, from Santiago to Havana, and from seventh grade to twelfth . . .

I sit down at last in a comfortable conference room with half a dozen pupils who—with one exception—are fourteen or fifteen years of age and all in the ninth grade. As usual, in my dialogue with pupils, our conversation is primarily in English; whenever necessary to prevent misunderstanding Martha rapidly fills in a word or phrase.

Marisela is fourteen: tall and slender, somewhat British in appearance, her long blond hair combed straight and parted in the middle. She begins, at my request, to tell me the details of her academic schedule. Every pupil in the ninth grade, she explains, must take ten subjects: Math, Spanish, English, History, Geography, Chemistry, Physics, Labor Education, Physical Education, Fundamentals of Political Knowledge.

Mario is thirteen years old but already in the ninth grade. Very small, with curly hair, he seems to be adored by all the rest. I ask him to run down some of the classes in more detail.

"In Labor Education," he replies, "we learn to work with tools of every kind. This year we are working with machine-tools—and primarily on metal. Last year we had practice with the same tools, but we worked with wood. The purpose is not to train us as *obreros* for a factory, although it may well be that some of us will choose that as the work of our career. The real purpose is that, when we are grown up, we will know exactly how to do that kind of work and we will have respect for those who do it as their livelihood, as well."

I ask him what he hopes to do, himself, when he grows up. He says that he would like to be an engineer. Marisela says the same. Two other girls, Emilia and Barbara, also plan to work as engineers. (I get the sense that "engineer" has somehow come to be contagious in

167

the group this week. If I were to come back in December, I would not be startled to discover that they all intended to be botanists or architects instead.) One student only, out of the full group—a vibrant, politically ferocious girl named Sandra—tells me she intends to work "within the political cadres of the military." Traditional sex-roles for young women at this school have pretty well gone by the board.

Sandra fills me in, at my request, on several other points about curriculum: "Most of our subjects are equally hard. Chemistry is perhaps a bit more tough, because we start organic chemistry this year. That stuff is hard . . . In History we are looking at the course of World War Two."

Intrigued by this, I ask her how she sizes up the basic issues and the various allies. She gives a pretty much unyielding picture of the way it was: "It was the fascist side against the socialists and capitalists together. The fascist side was Mussolini and Hitler. [She does not speak about Japan.] The allies were the U.S.S.R.—they were most important of all anti-fascist forces in the war—and also Britain, Poland, France . . . and the United States." She adds: "The Soviet Union made the greatest sacrifice in lives. The U.S. joined the war but also made enormous profit at the same time. A lot of people in the U.S. made an awful lot of money from the war."

I interrupt to ask for any comments about Hitler and receive from Mario this brief reply: "Hitler was a racist, but his racism was capricious. He hated dark-haired people with dark eyes and all, yet he was himself a little man with black hair and no blue eyes at all. He was *not* one of his own blond gods!"

Every time that Mario speaks, I look at him with slight surprise: "Did you just say 'capricious'?"

"Hitler *was* capricious," he replies.

I swallow my thoughts about this—and proceed to ask about the course on "Fundamentals . . ."

Again Mario, the sole boy in the group, jumps right in and rattles off the answer, buzzing like a bee into my ear: "Marx, Engels, Lenin, Hegel . . . This is the basic reading-matter for the year."

I ask about Hegel, since that sounds more than a little difficult for junior high. Sandra bounces back with an unhesitant reply: "We don't read *all* that Hegel wrote! That would take a hundred years! We just read excerpts: parts that help us understand."

"How do you feel about the parts of Hegel that you know?"

Sandra: "Hegel was against the capitalist system— but, in my belief, for the wrong reasons."

After this brisk summary of Hegel I attempt to step back into less ambitious subject-matter for a while. I ask if somebody would give me a quick rundown on their daily schedule. "Not Sandra or Mario," I say. "Somebody else!"

Emilia—seemingly shy until this time, a serious-looking girl with dark black bangs—takes up the burden and becomes a lot less shy. A little like Minister Fernández, she runs down the schedule with machine-gun speed: "We're up at six, do wake-up exercises, clean our rooms, and have breakfast at seven. After breakfast, there's a brief assembly outside where we hear the news and lots of interesting things. We go to class at seven twenty if we're in the seventh grade or ninth. Eighth graders do their fieldwork in the morning—their schedule is the same, but just the other way around. After we attend five classes, we have lunch around twelve thirty but we get one break at ten fifteen for sweets and for soft drinks. The dining-hall closes at twelve forty-five. Then we go out to the fields. We don't march! *Please do not say that we march.* But we line up and we file. Teachers go with us, but our guides out in the fields are older women—campesinas—from the farms close to the school."

I ask if it gets real hot out there all day long in the sun?

Sandra, despite my efforts, interrupts. "Just a little—not too bad. Even *you* could probably get used to it in time . . ."

I ask them what they grow. Emilia picks things up again and fires back: "Mainly beets . . . also bananas . . . but we grow crops in rotation now, so that the land will be in use. Therefore, we plant potatoes, too. The campesinas do the planting of banana trees—to show us how. It is a delicate job. We do the work of stripping off the leaves, but not the planting of the trees."

I ask what I consider an innocent question—"Why can't students do the planting also?"—and am instantly shot down.

Sandra, who appears all set to sit in Rosario García's chair, as soon as she resigns or, if need be, to take the military burdens from Raúl Castro in a pinch, gives it to me in no uncertain terms. "Listen! This is an important crop for export! It isn't something to play with. It's for real. We expect a good crop this year, both for use at home and export. We export to many different nations, as you ought to know by now."

Emilia finishes the schedule of the day, and thereby gets me off the hook: "At four thirty we come back and bathe. At five thirty we line up to go to quiet study. Twice a week it's individual study. Three times a week we work in teams so we can help each other. Supper is at seven thirty, then free time for recreation, meetings and those things. At ten o'clock we go back to our dorms to wash and then we go to sleep."

I ask if everyone gets sufficient sleep. Mario, almost beneath my shoulder at this point, answers back: "It has been foreseen that this is just exactly the amount of sleep we need."

Growing more accustomed to his quite astonishing vocabulary, I notice the hour and I try to press ahead with my last questions. I ask the students to define the meaning of "freedom" in the terms they find correct. I say that "freedom" at Kent State in Ohio came very close to meaning "free speech."

Sandra shoots right back with one of her no-nonsense definitions: "Freedom means—when you are free from *international capitalistic exploitation!*"

I plug a little for freedom of speech. At first only one student, Barbara, who has been almost entirely silent up to now, concedes a bit of value here. "Freedom of speech is going to be important if you want to try to build up solidarity among the people in a land that is oppressed." She adds, however: "Guns are quicker, though."

Sandra, oddly more conciliatory now, all at once surprises me by her agreement with my point of view: "In order to build up solidarity the people need to share their views. So they *do* need, of course, to have free speech."

When I ask the crucial question, though, I run right into a stone wall: "Do you have free speech in Cuba now?"

"We don't perceive that as a useful question," Mario replies. "In our society we are *already* free from exploitation now."

He speaks to me in didactic terms, as if I were (and as I *am*, in his view) a slow learner: "After the Spanish War was nearly won, the U.S. sent the battleship *Maine*, then blew it up as a pretext to attack the Spaniards and to come into the war. We had been warned of intervention of this kind. José Martí wrote, twenty years before, that this would be the sequence of events."

Barbara: "There was treachery by the rulers of the

U.S.A. Soon they started exploitation of our people—indirectly."

"First indirect—then *direct!*" says Sandra. "The U.S. corporations took our land. Machado, San Martín, Batista . . . they were puppets for the U.S.A."

I ask again, "To end all this . . . is freedom?"

They start to explain to me about the former exploitation in Angola. I recognize their earnest effort to instruct me about something (i.e., exploitation) which, because I press the other point, they are convinced I do not understand.

To end the matter, I report to them the truth: I happen to agree with their position on the exploitation of Angola. They seem relieved at last, as if I'm not so stupid as I seem.

I press on to another question. It is a point about the differential which still exists in Cuba between salaries for workers and those which are granted to professionals like doctors. I offer the example of an average Cuban worker, infinitely better off, of course, than he or she has ever been before (apart from everything else, because at least they really *do* have work) but nonetheless with monthly earnings of 140 pesos (U.S. $175). A doctor, on the other hand, earns between 600 and 900 pesos a month. "Why should some folks get so much—and poor folks so much less?"

Sandra neatly aims and shoots me down once more—as if I were a C-47 circling in the sky above the school: "We don't have poor people in Cuba, as you know quite well, so your question isn't stated very well. If you think those workers in our factories are poor, then you can't even *dream* what poverty was like."

I tell her she is right. "My words were careless, but you still don't seem to have the nerve to deal with the real point."

"What *is* it?" she asks, as if she barely can put up with me by now.

"Workers earn 140 pesos. Doctors earn at least 600 pesos. The difference seems too great."

She thinks about it—and, once again to my surprise, agrees: "I have to admit it—I think you're right. They both work hard. The difference is too great. As history advances we'll reduce that disproportion. Someday, everyone who works as hard as possible should get the same."

Marisela bites her lip, looks hard into the air, then says: "I don't agree. The doctor has studied longer. What he does contributes more. I don't believe a factory worker deserves the same."

They argue back and forth about this issue. It soon becomes apparent that the gulf that separates them is profound. (I wonder that they have not spoken of this point before.) The clock, by now, reads well past twelve. I soon will have to go.

I try to wind things up with a traditional but rather soporific question: "Would you like to send along suggestions for those students who are just about your age in the United States?"

Everyone looks at someone else, as if they need to settle on a common point of view. There is a kind of huddle and then Mario replies. "Tell them, please, that we support them in their fight against their rulers—whoever they are—the corporations or the CIA. We do not suggest, however, that they think about the use of weapons. They cannot use weapons, because of their situation and their age. We would advise them first to read more books about important struggles like Moncada. We would advise them to read speeches of Fidel and also, of course, to read the works of Che . . . We would advise them also to read books by Marx and Engels . . ."

Mario goes on with his selective reading-list. It is a list that would not be bizarre to certain groups of U.S. students, maybe three or four years older, if it were a decade back . . .

When he is done, I check their ages and the spelling of their names one final time. Sandra says: "I bet that you will find it easy to remember mine! It's just the same as Sandra Scheuer—who died beneath the rifles at Kent State."

She shakes my hand and squeezes it so hard I am afraid it will fall off. The others also shake my hand. In the awkward moment of goodbye, Sandra tousles Mario's hair, and everybody smiles. The group reminds me of a little team. It was their huddle that brought that thought to mind, but I have felt it all along.

Sandra says, "You would be welcome to come back and talk with us some more. It isn't bad, you know, to disagree."

The principal returns in time to hear her final comment and he laughs out loud when she suggests that I could come back if I want. He puts his hand protectively over my shoulder.

"I *will* be back . . . I will be back on Monday," I reply.

Monday morning: I find waiting in readiness for my arrival the same team to which, on Friday, I had said what they first took to be a last goodbye. There is, however, the addition of another boy (named Stefan) and a girl (named Leonora).

I plunge right off into unfinished business. I ask about career plans once again. Stefan, it turns out, wants to be "a middle-level chemical technician." Leonora's interest is in "theater, languages, and dance."

Interested in Leonora's choice, I ask her, "Is your choice one which will be of use to Cuba? Or is it one which will be of use, first of all, to *you?* Which comes first: your own wish, or the interests of the state?"

"I would deeply wish," says Leonora, "to be able to dance and sing and to perform on stage for all the years of my career. I do not really think, however, that this would be fair. There are so many other boys and girls who have the skills to sing and dance but need a teacher in their schools to help them to attain the training to develop in those skills. I love the stage. Theater is beautiful. In other situations, if it were a simple matter, there would be no question of my choice, but in this situation it has become my choice to study as a teacher and to help young people learn the foreign languages to go abroad to Europe to learn to be great artists who can then perform throughout the world. I believe that this is the right choice. I also think it is my obligation in the revolution."

Her voice is crystalline, musical, and clear. There is a moment of long silence in the room. I think of Christina, child of the literacy revolution—and her longing also to perform on stage, to sing and dance. I jot down a reminder to myself: It seems the sense of obligation to "the others"—or, as some say it, "in the revolution"— is an overriding theme in almost every conversation of this kind. I jot down, also, on the pad of paper in my hands, that people repeatedly make use of the term, "the revolution," as if it were a synonym for "government" or "state." Pupils seem to find it natural to speak about their role, position, obligation, not "to the government," but "in the revolution." There are a good many differences, I feel, between the implications of this term and all that is connoted by a sense of obligation "to the state."

I ask Mario, "Do you feel the right to choose whatever work you like the best?"

"I have the right to choose my own career," he quietly replies, "but it should be in close accord with the most urgent needs of all the people. We cannot always follow up the work of our first choice."

Nobody here has chosen manual work of any kind as a career. "If this is so—what you have said—why didn't any of you choose to be a farmer or *obrero?* Surely the government needs good workers too."

"We will do what the revolution asks," says Leonora. It is a finalizing answer. I can sense the team will fight me to the wall if I pursue this point, so I move on to something new:

"When you think about history during your work at school what does the word seem to suggest to you? What does it mean?" I asked this question once to senior high school students in Schenectady. The answers all were of one kind: "History is everything that happened in the past and is now over . . . History is cycles . . . processes . . . inevitable patterns . . . History is what is done by serious and important people . . ."

The answers I receive this time are equally uniform, but in a different way:

"Through history we see the origins of our country," Marisela starts to say. "It is the past, but there are things that we do now which will be part of history someday."

When she says "we," I ask her if she means the students right here in this room. "The people change history," she says. "The masses . . . We are only a part of the masses in this room."

I find Marisela a lucid and extremely earnest girl. I press her a bit: "Can just one man, or just one woman, sometimes turn the tide?"

"No," she replies. "Only with the help of the masses can we ever turn the tide."

"How would you reach the masses if you needed to?" I ask.

"We would go to one of our groups: the UJC, the

176

FMC, the CDR . . . I would, myself, go to the FMC."

I try very briefly to get them to speak of women's rights. I ask the students if they ever study women of the past—or mostly men.

"For a long time," says Sandra, "women were not in positions to assert themselves. Nowadays in our country we can take an equal stand. So reading in the past means mainly reading about men. But I can tell you one thing: It won't be that way for long!"

"Who are some of the women whom you most admire?"

Three names come back in rapid sequence . . . Lidia Doce (a young Cuban woman who was killed in action during the fight to overthrow Batista) . . . Allison Krause (who died at Kent State) . . . Tania . . .

I ask the obvious. "What do they have in common?"

"All," says Marisela, "gave their lives for their beliefs."

I ask her, therefore, what is, of course, a set-up question: "Isn't life *itself* the most important thing in life?"

All at once the little room explodes with voices.

Stefan: "Progress is more important, in my belief."

Marisela: "Justice is more important, also."

Mario: "Freedom is clearly more important."

For the last time I press that button that infuriates so many children in the team. "What is it, just exactly, that you have in mind when you use a word like freedom?"

Sandra, in a very loud voice: *"When there is exploitation, I have told you already—then the people are not free!"*

"Is Cuba free?"

"You know it is!" says Sandra.

"Is the Soviet Union free?"

"Of course!" She has assumed the burden of my education once again.

"Is there freedom in the U.S.A.?"

Sandra (no hesitation): *"No!"*

"How can you be so positive?" I ask.

She fires it right back: *"If freedom existed in the U.S.A., then racism would not."*

I have the sudden thought that she will strangle me if I pursue the point, so I give up at last.

The final question that I raise within this group and in this school pertains to a matter that I have intentionally postponed for now. It is a matter which I cannot conscionably pass by and yet which I know very well is likely to cause discontent or even to invite some fury.

"I would like to wind things up today by asking you one question that has bothered me since I first came to Cuba. In general I think you do believe that I have come to feel great admiration both for the Cuban revolution and especially for the work that has been done in education with the adults and now with young people, too, as in this school right here. Still, I try to find some things that someone in your education system may wish to correct. There is one problem that I think about a lot. It is the fact that all your books, newspapers, magazines, tell exactly the same side of every issue and, in certain cases, leave out things that seem to me of real importance. I could add one point to that by saying that I tend to share the views that are presented in the Cuban press, especially when there is a reprint of a lecture by Fidel. I love to read those speeches and I love to read the way the audience responds.

"Sometimes, however, *Granma* and the afternoon paper seem to me a little dull. To be quite honest, I don't think that they print a lot of news and not enough opinions or enough long feature stories in these papers. Wouldn't it be a good idea, therefore, to get some foreign papers—so that you could get a lot more information and also hear a lot of different points of view?"

Again, the students whisper to each other very

briefly, then quietly sit back while one of them—Mario, once more—begins to speak.

"For me," he says, "I don't feel that I need to see the U.S. press, if it is *that* 'foreign' press you have in mind. We quote long sections from *The New York Times* in *Granma.*"

"The only items from the U.S. press that I have seen in *Granma* are the ones that show the bad side of my nation. There is a lot of stuff you never get to see because it says something that's good about the U.S.A."

I feel uneasy taking up this role, since I know very well that Cuban kids and adults both have plenty of reason to express a grave distrust of the United States. Still, for the sake of provocation, I persist: "There's been some talk about competing in baseball with each other. Why not have a taste of competition of the press as well?"

"Do the students of the U.S.A. read *Granma?*" Mario asks. Sandra puts her arm around his neck and kisses him on the cheek as his reward.

"Do students in Ohio read *The New York Times?*" she asks.

"No. They don't. Not at your age, for sure. But just because our students miss the chance to face some challenges, why should Cuban students have to miss them too?"

Mario says: "We are convinced our papers tell the truth. We don't believe that they exaggerate or that they tell us lies about the U.S. Maybe by error—that could always be the case. In general, in the issues that count, like racist murders and the shootings at Kent State and all the crimes of Richard Nixon and the CIA, I think we get the truth."

Sandra adds one final point which Mario has ignored. "About the extra stuff that we don't know—the extra stories in your papers that you say we do not have—we don't need to read newspapers for the sake of entertainment. We would rather read the paper for the news and then for our pleasure we can go and read good books."

The principal, who has entered the room, now quietly observes, "Whenever the U.S. government interferes in foreign lands, it tries to win the people of your country by denial and deceit. Sometimes your papers are willing to expose these lies, but usually they don't, until too late. They do sensational exposés—right *after* all the dirty work is done! Playa Girón is one example. The murder of Allende is another. Why should the press in the United States expose the actions of the CIA until the goal is won? Who owns those papers after all? Who pays the money for the campaigns for your president's election? They are the same people—or the friends of the same people. Why should they undercut their own self-interest? The people of the U.S. think they have a competitive press. Except for insignificant radical and progressive journals, this is not the case. The big press and TV in the U.S.A. compete for sales and for advertisements, and they can do that by sensational stories about things that do not matter, or else things that *do*—but are all *done*. They don't compete in serious ideas. They are all capitalists and they believe that it is quite correct to go into a Third World nation to exploit both the people and the land.

"The U.S. press would not accept that Cuba went to join the struggle in Angola. Your papers spoke of 'foreign intervention'—after Vietnam! We were invited by the grass-roots elements of Angola, not by a puppet dictator that U.S. agents set up in Saigon!"

He becomes increasingly heated as he talks: "The issue in Angola was not 'foreign intervention' for the U.S. press. The issue was that we are socialists and so too are the people's leaders whom we went to help and whom we plan to *keep on helping* with their schools and hospitals and every other thing they need! The U.S. possibly would like to have extracted natural resources from Angola. Well, you have missed your chance . . ."

It seems fair that after so much time the principal of this school should have a chance to have his say. He is an intense, intelligent man of twenty-six—Jorge del Balle is his name. He is consistently polite to me, despite the fervor of his words.

I ask him, "If it is true that the U.S. press is full of lies, why be afraid to let your pupils know? Why be afraid of papers that are full of lies? Won't it show through?"

"No," he says, "that isn't the real issue. Of course, we're not afraid of lies. The point is, honestly, that we just can't afford to waste the time."

"That's one point that I forgot," says Mario, sitting beside me.

"When we are working so hard to build socialism," the principal goes on, "when we are working night and day—as you see very well, and as I am convinced you understand—we don't have time to look at everything from fifteen different points of view! It is also honest to tell you that it makes our work more difficult to have our views distorted and our children's minds confused with a lot of clever lies, especially when they are surrounded by advertisements for elegant things which we are still too poor to buy! It is too much! It is unfair! You ask me a hard question, so I give you a hard answer. It is the truth; we find it very difficult to answer in your terms. We are working so hard! We don't read the Soviet press or Eastern European publications either. What do we read? We read the news, eight little pages worth! That's all we get! And then we read our physics books and after that we read Charles Dickens and *Tom Sawyer,* too!"

The children are silent. Even Sandra seems to feel the power of her principal's convictions. I did not come here, however, in order to see how well I can debate. I came, rather, to find out what a certain number of Cuban students and their teachers honestly believe. In this respect I feel I have achieved my goal.

So, once again, as on the day before, we end our talk with lots of heat and maybe no more light than when we first began. Ten days more, as I know well, would never solve these questions. It would take, at the very least, ten years . . .

It is lunchtime once again; but this time it is not at all the same as on last Friday. This time as I say goodbye there is the recognition that it is, for now at least, "goodbye for good." The students know that this time I will not be back to chat, infuriate, and vie with them tomorrow. Within two days, as I explain, I will be on a nonstop flight to Montreal. Soon after, I will be at home in the United States.

"To Montreal!" says Sandra. She sounds genuinely alarmed. "How many hours does that plane trip take?"

"Almost five," I tell her, dreading every minute of that ride already.

"Five hours!" she says. "You're taking a long ride . . ."

Something is different now: something like the changes in the air before a storm. I ask one question. "Would you like me to carry home a message to the mothers and the fathers of the students who were killed that day out on the hillside at Kent State?"

Sandra answers—and her voice is startlingly soft. "Tell them," she says, "that we remember . . . that we always will remember . . . that we are sorry for their suffering . . . that we will always be beside them in their pain." After a pause, she swallows hard to speak these simple words: "And tell them, please, we send our love."

I tell her that I will keep my promise and we all stand

up. The group of us, somehow, after two days of debate, have come to be close friends. As the car leaves they stand on the front steps. I study them a moment so that I will not forget. I memorize the faces of each one. It is so hard to tell myself this is the last goodbye.

IV

The voices and the faces of Emilia, Marisela, Mario and Sandra remain so vivid in my memory today that it is easy to forget that this school is only one of what will soon be six or seven hundred of such schools.

Meanwhile, in the midst of all of this exhilaration, it also seems important not to bypass one significant alternative to the schools *en campo*, one which constitutes a major pedagogic option for increasing numbers of young boys and girls in Cuba after they complete their first six years of school.

That option is to go—not to the country—but to one of two extremely large and academically demanding schools, urban in location and technically designated as vocational schools—institutions, however, which are so distinct from all traditional images of that type of school in the United States as to seem to justify another designation altogether.

Woodwork, shop, second-rate math and language classes, third-rate science, social science, and the rest—

as we have come to know this kind of school too well in the United States—have nothing to do with the two "schools of vocation" already in full operation within Cuba and the twelve now being planned.

The schools are viewed as every bit the match, in academic terms, of those six hundred schools *en campo* that have been the pride of Minister Fernández. Both have six-year programs, starting in the seventh grade and ending in the twelfth. They are large schools, almost academic cities, accommodating ten or twelve times the enrollment of each school *en campo*.

The newest of the two has been in operation for exactly one year, since September 1977. It is dedicated to José Martí and situated in one of the newly created eastern provinces, Holguín—an area that contains one of the richest sources of raw nickel in the world, as well as an ultramodern refinery at Moa Bay, expropriated by the Cuban government from Freeport Sulphur. (Holguín is pretty much the northeast third of what was once the vast and sprawling Oriente Province).

The school, whose land and buildings together occupy four hundred and ten thousand square meters, offers its forty-five hundred pupils a staff of fifteen hundred teachers, coaches, cooks and counselors, doctors, nurses, sub-directors, principals, and parent-aides, seventy-five classrooms, twenty-six labs for chemistry, physics and biology (one of the special fields of concentration in the school is hemochemistry), eight studios for artists, twenty-four rooms for art instruction, two mini-theaters, one large theater to show films and plays, twenty-four rooms for student clubs and such, a data-processing center for the use of students (one which makes use of third-generation Soviet computers), three libraries (one for books, one for periodicals, and one for music), two reading rooms permitting quiet conversation, two reading rooms for silent study, four rooms for seminars, twenty-eight rooms for faculty and other staff, a natural-sciences museum, a forty-seven-bed hospital, three outdoor pools, a gym, two tennis courts, two handball courts, ten basketball courts, ten volleyball courts, two baseball fields, two fields for track and soccer, eleven dormitories of four stories each—and a kitchen and dining-hall equipped to serve six thousand meals three times each day.

I have attempted in this book to speak only of schools and classes I have visited in person. In this one case, I have been obliged to trust the press reports: I have not yet had a chance to visit and observe the classes at the Martí School. I have described the school, in any case, because I think the mere statistics of this pedagogic complex are so far beyond all notions previously conveyed by words such as "vocational education" as to merit even second-hand report.

The western counterpart of the Martí School is in Havana Province. It is called the Lenin School and it is situated less than fifteen miles from the city of Havana. This is a school I feel I know firsthand, having spent a long and interesting day both in its classes and in its working center. The Lenin School, established first in 1966, rebuilt to offer broader services to pupils during 1972, and now expanded once again, serves the same number of pupils as the Martí School, although with fewer buildings, meeting rooms, athletic facilities, "a-v centers" and other special features—but with only slightly less impressive class and lab facilities. Here, as at the Martí School, students and faculty divide the day between hard academic study and productive labor. The school has a drop-out rate of less than two percent.

The Lenin School bears a reputation in Havana somewhat like those of Bronx Science, Exeter, or Groton. Many of its graduates go to universities in Prague, Moscow, Budapest, Berlin, or Warsaw. In spite of the academic pace, however, I did not at any time while I was in this school experience that sense of anguish, as of reliving a bad dream, that hits me almost every time I walk into the hallways and begin to breathe the smell of chalk dust and dead air of almost any secondary school in the United States.

Some of this reduction in the customary tension and anxiety of public school (for me) is probably the consequence of language differences, of tropical climate, and the strangeness of milieu; but I am convinced there is another, more substantial reason for that difference too: If I can trust my own internal sense of relaxation first and, after that, the cheerful, energetic, and fast-stepping spirit that pervades the corridors and breezeways of the school, then I am tempted to suggest that something here is really different. There is a sense of shared achievement—hard work that remains at all times one good notch below the level of competitive obsession—and, always too, a willingness to laugh, and tease, and play, especially to tease *oneself*.

Classes at the Lenin School, as in most secondary schools of Cuba, begin at approximately seven thirty. Students spend a little more than half the day in academic preparation, with excellent instruction in the social sciences and the humanities. The older students that I met in class spoke (and could read) English with both accuracy and good pronunciation. Primary emphasis, however, is on science, with special interest in a core curriculum of TV, computer science, radio, and electronics.

That portion of the day which is not given up to academic work is spent within a working center, intentionally constructed as one section of the school itself, which manufactures almost all the radios, TV antennas, and small dry-cell batteries in use in Cuba. (Figures for 1976 indicate that the school's production of two models of transistor radio in that year alone was fifty thousand.)

There is a waiting-list of those who would, as they have said to me, give almost anything to get admitted to the school. Roberto Retamár, a well known Cuban poet, editor of *Casa* and former Yale professor, told me of his daughter's admission as if she had just been accepted by New England's most exclusive prep school.

The school's attraction is not hard to understand. There are very few schools in North America or Europe which seem to have been able to combine with so much skill a reverence for productive labor and an impressive level of true humanistic education of "the whole man" and "whole woman." The factory work requires skill; but it does not seem overly exhausting. It is, moreover, supervised with scrupulous care by teachers, doctors, nurses, veteran factory workers and the like.

The course of study resembles closely that which I have summarized already for the Kent and Che Guevara schools. In twelfth-grade English class, I asked the students what they liked the most to read when they were given a free choice. Answers ranged from Hemingway (the first selection in almost every case) to Shakespeare, Thackeray, Dickens—and, in several cases, the novels and polemics of Jack London or of Upton Sinclair. Outside one classroom on an open shelf, three or four copies of Boccaccio's *Decameron* were waiting for someone's intellectual interest—or else, perhaps, just left there in a hurry by some pupils on the way to class.

Of all the schools that I have visited in Cuba, none—other than Martyrs of Kent—ever has impressed me in the same way as the Lenin School. Vocational education has a very long way to go in Europe and in North America, as well, before it has a chance to catch up with the practical vision of this artful institution.

V

In the schools of Cuba it seems possible to view almost the whole society in microcosm. This is the case because so much of what goes on within those schools, to borrow Sandra's words, "isn't something to play with —it's for real." Despite its impressive pedagogic buildings, Cuba, in an interesting sense, has "de-schooled" the whole idea of school, by breaking the shell, the glaze, the plastic lacquer, that divides a "school deed" from a real deed, a "school day" from a real day—or a "school year" from real life.

Thus, for example, even the highly specialized polytechnic schools of Cuba do not allow the customary unreality, the distance, the postponement of adult responsibility and concurrent satisfaction identified with schools in almost every nation for more than one hundred years, to undercut the children's sense of purchase on hard, practical applications of the things they learn.

More than one of our familiar expectations of the limits and parameters of institutions known as "public schools" fall by the way when we walk into any one of these exciting, active, "part-of-the-real-world" places, still defined as "school" within the lexicon of Cuban educators, but unlike anything that "school" has ever meant before.

The one example I would like to offer here is a polytechnic school which does *not* boast high college-entrance scores, one indeed which does not exist to educate its students for a university career, but rather trains its pupils to be highly skilled technicians in one quite specific and essential field.

The school is named Martínez Villena. It began in 1964 as the Institute of Fertilizers and of Animal Nutrition. Today, it functions as the pedagogic wing of one of the most modern animal-breeding institutes in Cuba— an institute whose land it shares and whose facilities it partially operates and helps to staff. Simultaneously, it educates twelve hundred Cuban girls and boys. Its students have in every case already completed lower-level secondary. They come here, therefore, as an alternative to those three years which otherwise would have been designated as *pre-universidad*. The age-span is fifteen to eighteen years.

The school is physically and architecturally delightful and it is here that Fidel Castro often comes in search of respite during periods of strain, or else to check on how the students—as well as certain of his favorite cows— are doing.

The classes are of great interest in themselves, but it is the experimental dairy in particular, with its intricate animal technology, that commands my interest. I tell the principal, therefore, that I would be glad to bypass the familiar business of class visits in order to spend more time out in the fields and in the dairy-stalls.

Within minutes a young man who is a last-year student at the school is strolling with me toward a row of "breeding stations." He is seventeen. His name is Alejandro. He seems almost to be exploding with statistics, numbers, explanations. Some of what he says, especially at first, goes way beyond all outer realms of anything that I could possibly understand. Most of his talk, however, is entirely comprehensible and is presented with painstaking care.

"The familiar breed of cattle now traditional in Cuba is well fitted to the climate but does not produce sufficient milk or meat. Milk is our major interest, so we now are introducing new breeds—chiefly Holstein and Swiss Brown—in order to arrive at an effective cross, while trying at the same time to develop better silage processes. Our country has twelve months of sun to grow the grass but does not have sufficient rain. In recent years especially we have had to undergo long periods of drought.

"Breeding," he continues—as we walk along the path before a series of bright-looking whitewashed "houses" (each of which provides the sanctuary of one animal or more)—"is done primarily by artificial methods of insemination. Immediate production rates are less important to us than the scientific progress we can make. We are investing many of our hopes, right now, in the cattle-breed F-1. It is a mixed breed: Céboul with Red Holstein. We also are investigating different types of grass. You have probably noticed that we don't use silos here, as in the U.S., but a horizontal silage method with molasses that has been compressed into the grass to guarantee it will not rot. The type of grass in which we have the greatest interest is Bermuda Cross."

I ask him if it is British—possibly the product of a research project at an agricultural center in Bermuda.

"No," he answers. "It is just a name, Bermuda Cross. To give your *compañeros* proper credit, it is a grass that first was tested out in Gainesville. We discover that it serves our needs quite well."

Apart from his knowledge of breeding and of silage, Alejandro also has a large supply of information on the milking and maternity procedures.

"This," he says, as we enter a white and cheerful stable with a grassy "bed" surrounded by all sorts of Swiss-made scientific apparatus, "is the place the cows are taken when they go into labor. It is an ultramodern laboratory to assure the most secure and sterile processes. We speak of it as 'the maternity ward.'"

Next door, I see the logical follow-up: "the pediatric ward." It is a sparkling room in which the newborn calves are fed and maintained at a wholesome temperature.

Finally, Alejandro shows me one of the Swiss-built milking stations. "Before the revolution, with the old breed, we were content if each cow could produce as much as 1.5 or maybe 1.8 milk-liters in a day. By 1976 each cow at this school was producing 7.6. This, however, due to our continual experimentation on the farm, may be somewhat low. The average yield in Cuba as a whole is possibly a little higher. There are some cows, of course, which yield as much as twelve or fifteen liters in a day."

It is easy, while listening to Alejandro, to forget that he is speaking not of an isolated scientific institute, designed and supervised by graduates of Berkeley, Iowa, or M.I.T., but of a breeding center which is simultaneously a polytechnic school that serves twelve hundred teenage pupils.

The grass I see, thrown into the cattle-pens, was thrown there by boys and girls sixteen years old. The immaculate young men and women who pet, comfort, and milk the cows in those bright modern stalls are sixteen years old, too. The workers who hose out the blood and afterbirth in the "maternity ward" and then go next door to play with the young calves are adolescents also.

All of this poses a vivid contrast to the artificial ("simulation") character of much of the day-to-day routine of public schools in North America. In the U.S. we often spend ten million dollars to construct expensive secondary schools in ghetto neighborhoods, cut off from the real world even in concrete terms—by lack of windows. Then the principal goes out to spend ten thousand dollars more to buy a "simulation game" called "Ghetto," by means of which the children may be able to experience (or simulate) that on-going world of truth and pain in which they *live* but which their schools have, at so high a cost, shut out of sight.

I have come to think of this as the simulation factor. (Some kids that I know describe it as the "as-if" factor.) Our schools, as Whitehead long ago observed, are built to start with on "inert ideas"—ideas that lead to nothing, not to action, not to passion, not to transformation, but (at most) to good term papers and examinations. Childhood thereby becomes a moratorium on life. It is a time in which young people spend about one third of their projected biological existence in preparation for that two thirds they may never live to know. This may well be one of the major reasons why the years in junior high school, for our children, prove so frequently to be both tedious and unreal.

Secondary schools such as Martínez Villena do not have to struggle with dilemmas of this kind. The schools are based, from start to finish, on a firm and vivid grasp upon the concrete truths of life itself. Almost all ideas and skills that are acquired in these schools are meant to lead to actions, to real work, and to real dedication, not twenty years hence, nor even twelve, but here and now in the period in which the children work and live.

I have referred before to a quotation from José Martí: "Properly speaking, we should not talk of schools at all, but we should speak of schools as workshops for real life." There are many ideas within the Cuban schools that serious and reflective U.S. citizens will not find to their own taste; but it would serve even the skeptics well, I think, to take a good look at the words of this prophetic man, and at the concept of idea-and-labor, study-and-the-plow, which makes it needless to bring simulation games into the Cuban public schools—because the real world is already there.

VI

It remains to comment briefly on the classroom atmosphere in Cuba and the relationship between pupil and teacher. Certainly the style of the Cuban classroom teacher is a good deal less free-flowing, less spontaneous, than in many of the innovative schools here in the U.S.

Nonetheless, it seems to me that the present amalgam of the old and new achieved by Cuban educators in the course of almost twenty years is not just realistic in the terms of Cuba's actual needs but possibly an excellent example for those people in our public schools who are bewildered by our failure to teach basic skills, yet do not wish to see our teachers going back to the archaic practices of thirty years before. There is a third way: neither fatuous nor dictatorial, neither whimsical and aimless nor tyrannical. It is a way that has far more to do with teacher personality than with the newest gadgets or with printed texts.

Someplace between Summerhill and Eton (and maybe

a little closer to the second than the first), the end result is order reconciled with polite irreverence; hard work, with an impressive wish to help and share; hard skills, wedded to a direct knowledge of their possible productive or aesthetic applications.

There is another facet of the Cuban schools that seems to me to merit brief reiteration: If the conversations that I held in both the Kent and the Guevara schools *en campo* offer any clear example, it seems to be one of children who do not perceive themselves as either objects or spectators of historic process. Cuban pupils, helped certainly by the onrush of political events on every side and influenced also by continual reminders of the revolutionary activism of the Great Campaign, appear to grow up with the satisfying sense of being part of history: energetic colleagues and "collaborators" in the process of its revolutionary transformation.

Whenever children can comfortably speak, as Leonora did, about "my obligation in"—not "to"—the revolution; when Carlos can say, "If it is true . . ., it is a fact for which I feel great shame. I will find out"; when Sandra can say, of women's secondary role in history, that "it won't be that way for long," it seems to me a tragic and debilitating aspect of the public school as we have known it for one hundred years has been substantially transcended.

The Cuban government has—quite properly, in my belief—achieved immense esteem in pedagogic circles not only for its rapid gains in wiping out illiteracy among its adult population but also for its great success in breaking down that plastic shell that has eternally encased the institution known as "public school" in almost every nation of the earth.

There are these words in the Bible: "Where there is no vision, the people perish." In Cuban schools, unlike almost all others I have seen in various sections of the world, the vision is strong, the dream is vivid and the goal is clear. There is a sense, within the Cuban schools, that one is working for a purpose and that that purpose is a great deal more profound and more important than the selfish pleasure of an individual reward. The goal is to become an active member in a common campaign to win an ethical objective. Nothing could be more unlike the atmosphere of "Sunday afternoon neurosis," identified in the writings of Paul Goodman as the chronic sickness of the average (U.S.) public school.

If, in addition to the vision and the sense of purpose that I have described above, the Cuban schools can also manage (which also means to dare) to give their pupils an unstinting flow of strong, competitive ideas, if such a flow of strong, competitive ideas is not postponed forever in the name of siege conditions but if they soon appear to thrive, as well as merely to prevail, then it seems to me the nation and its schools will both win and deserve a very high degree of international esteem.

It would be naïve to say that Cuba has, at this point, come even close to reaching this ideal—or even that such a purpose represents a clear-cut and consensual goal among the leaders of the Cuban schools. A great deal still remains to be decided in the ten or fifteen years immediately ahead. I would like to think that millions of young people will turn out as conscientious, flexible, and non-dogmatic as Peter and Martha—or Abel Prieto. Peter's enthusiasm for "your Boston Symphony," Fernández's totally earnest, even wistful, yearning to attribute incorruptible character to Adlai Stevenson, despite his grim performance at the U.N. in the days after the Bay of Pigs—these generous qualities are those that I would hope to see repeated many million times during the years to come.

Much will depend upon the schools; and, in the Cuban case, the schools will count a great deal more than written press or radio/TV I am back, then, with the question that I first confronted in my final dialogue with Sandra, Mario, and Marisela.

Ideological bias is certain to persist within the Cuban schools, as in all public schools within all nations since the public schools began. Can there, at the same time, be a place, a role, and a respect, for an eternal rebel, an eternal nonconformist—one like Carlos . . . like Ferrer . . . or like Fidel?

How *did* Ferrer, we might well ask, become the eloquent, open-minded, and poetic revolutionary that I came to know? Not, surely, in a sheltered classroom— of whatever brand—but in an atmosphere, schoolhouse or not, in which ideas were fiery and the winds blew strong. The proliferation of such human beings as these is one risk, I should think, that Cuba does not need to view with great alarm.

"We believe that you will be better revolutionaries than we," said Fidel Castro to the brigadistas as they set off for the mountains on a pilgrimage that started back in 1961 and still goes on today. If Fidel's dream is someday to come true, if they are someday to be *better,* then the children of that revolution must begin at least by being not one bit the *worse,* whether in terms of politics or passion, whether in terms of revolutionary dedication or in breadth of intellectual access and unceasing openness to doubt.

If this is a cautious statement, it is a hard-earned caution. My impulse, in the face of what I feel and see and hear within the schools and streets of Cuba, is to throw all caution to the winds and to speak solely of the decent aspirations and the eloquent ideals that have already been made real.

In this book I have spoken of only one of those ideals: the will and power to give ethical, equal, and effective education to every citizen, regardless of that person's economic status or political affiliations.

In the case of Cuba, effectiveness in public education seems by far the easiest to confirm. Whether we judge by Cuba's triumph in the struggle to eradicate adult illiteracy, by technological progress, by classroom preparation in genetics, electronics, or statistics, or by the reverence which is shown for art, literature, and music in the Cuban schools, there seems no question but that quality has now almost caught up with quantity in Cuba's education scheme.

Effectiveness alone, however, does not measure up to the demands and expectations of a nation dedicated to the dreams of Che Guevara and José Martí. The patterns of reward for academic labor, as I have debated them at length with students at Martyrs of Kent, have to be considered also in a full appraisal of the ethical and economic consequences of the intellectual preparation offered to the Cuban population.

If the rewards for certain avenues of preparation far outstrip those of all the others, then we are forced to wonder whether this consideration will not be a primary factor in the choices pupils make as they progress from year to year and whether this will not subvert the model of the self-effacing man or woman Che Guevara held up as an ethical ideal.

It is apparent, for example, that the sheer material rewards for a career in medicine are very, very high in contrast to the earnings of a semi-skilled technician, and higher still in contrast to the earnings of an unskilled worker at a factory or on a farm. It is one thing to announce, as it was said to me so many times, that "individual achievement in this nation is respected always in an emulative sense," but it is another thing if certain groups of highly skilled professionals can win the privilege to eat in pleasant restaurants, spend weekends in delightful new hotels, and also find the funds to purchase air-conditioners, refrigerators, or TV—while others must accept a life of relatively unexciting and austere routine.

Compared to the United States, the range of salaries is very small indeed. It is also small in contrast to the gross extremes of misery and wealth that were the curse of Cuba for all its modern history prior to 1959. Furthermore, there is a large degree of equal privilege assured by virtue of the abolition or (as in Christina's case) drastic reduction of most housing rentals, as well as by provision of free health care for all people, free day-care, and free schooling costs—including the cost of meals and clothes, as well as books and travel and tuition for the pupils of the schools *en campo* and the other five-day boarding-schools such as José Martí. Admission, moreover, as we have seen, is strictly regulated to prevent the influence of parental power or prestige.

Even so, the persistent dangers of a potentially remorseless meritocracy remain. I see no means by which to balance out the efforts and the earnings, the delights and the extremes of physical effort in the swelter of intense humidity and heat, so long as salary differentials for the intellectual versus the manual labor of a Cuban citizen remain so great. Sandra said to me, in her heavy-throated voice: "I think you're right, the difference is too great. As history advances we'll reduce that disproportion. Someday, everyone who works as hard as possible should get the same."

It remains to be seen to what degree the socialist conscience of a child such as Sandra will find the means to bring the practical incentives into line with ethical ideals. It may well be that government leaders will, in time, no longer feel the obligation to conciliate or to reward, beyond a modest limit, those who already have their own reward in the ever-changing intellectual chal-

200

lenges and triumphs that cannot be separated from a certain number of sophisticated and complex careers. To add the economic bonus, too, and to do so four times over (as at present), does not seem in keeping with the words and goals of Cuba's revolutionary leaders.

There seems to me no question but that pupils such as Mario and Sandra are totally devoted to a process of increasingly egalitarian reward, but there is also Marisela, who made clear to everyone within that meeting-room that she did not agree. Marisela was eloquent also—a lovely, generous, and persuasive human being. So it remains to be discovered in the years to come whether the children of the revolution are thinking more like Marisela or like Sandra, whatever their reverence for the words of Cuba's heroines and heroes and the views which they espouse.

Another ethical index of a social order and of its educational system is the visible degree of equal access it affords—for example, by the abolition of discrimination in regard to race and sex. In reference to the first it is astonishing to me to recognize, despite all prior doubts, that Cuba has, in fact as well as reputation, come to be a nation which is almost entirely color-blind. My own best evidence proved to be my routine evening efforts at quick written recollections of the people I had met during the day. Often I would jot down ten or twenty characteristics of a child or a teacher or a principal whom I had met and chatted with that day—before it would occur to me to scribble down that he or she was white, black, or mulatto. Several times, I found that I could not recall.

To a large degree it has to be said that the emphasis of Abel Prieto on this point seems in retrospect to be disarmingly precise. Any social order that can help a well trained U.S. citizen to fail to recognize a detail of this kind clearly has managed to make a multitude of other factors both more memorable and more important than skin-color.

In regard to the rights of women it occurs to me that Sandra (and her older fellow-citizens in the classes of the FOC) said almost all there is to say. It is obvious that many years of self-deprecation on the part of women, as well as several centuries of absolute male domination, cannot be so rapidly erased as many Cuban men and women would like to be able to report. It's still unfair, as Sandra made quite clear; but, as she said, "I can tell you one thing: It won't be that way for long!"

Cuban women, without question, now have equal rights and equal status in the eyes of the law; they also shoulder equal burdens, such as late-hour duty (neighborhood patrol) within the vigilancia of the CDR. More than once, both in Havana and in Santiago, a woman on guard duty for the CDR would ask me, in a gentle but insistent manner, to tell her why I happened to be looking with so much persistent curiosity into a dark store-window in the early hours of the dawn.

For now, however, it is honest to say that women still are not afforded equal power and prestige with Cuban men, even in the face of the new, highly publicized and, in my own view, earnestly enacted Family Code and even despite the pleadings of Fidel.

One final criterion of the moral values of a new and revolutionary social order seems to me to be the way in which the government does, or does not, pay respect to older people. In Cuba old people are not easily relegated to the slag-heap of retirement homes and welfare checks. I think of the vitality and optimism of Juan de la Cruz. I think, too, of the words of Rosario García, herself moving now beyond the realm of middle age, who said to me: "There was a time when we were thinking mainly of the young . . . We sense today the very great untapped potential of the old, even the very, very old..."

Behind these words there is a dream, a principle, a powerful idea—one which has been voiced here also in the U.S. by Paul Goodman, who spoke often of the terrible wastage of the talents of old people. He argued in vain for the employment and the residence of older people in buildings where our infant children might be left in day-care programs while their mothers and their fathers go to work. In many neighborhoods of Cuba this idea is now a viable reality: not an official government "plan" or "program" or the like but just a natural idea that grows in practice and in popularity with every passing year.

At stake here is not just the need "to keep old people happy" in an active and regenerative state of mind. It is the whole idea of work itself as a redeeming and rewarding need for every human being. Small kids, in third-grade classes I have had the chance to visit, work meticulously, though at a modest pace, in a forty-five minute period during which they take small amounts of tea from large imported barrels and then stitch that tea, by a well regulated process, into little tea bags for the use of Cuba's population. The children do not work unduly hard, nor do they injure their backs or strain their arms. They simply take a small, and seemingly enjoyable, role in helping to provide one of the basic needs of their society.

From young to old, the principle is the same. Those who can contribute to the common good do what they can. It is impressive to perceive how much the little kids can do. Older people work with these small children to assist them in their task. I think again, while in this class, of the slogan popular back in 1961, during the literacy work: "Those who know, teach. Those who don't, learn."

The heritage of the Great Campaign lives on.

EPILOGUE

It seems, when U.S. citizens speak about Cuba to other U.S. citizens, the subject at hand can sometimes fall far out of view. I would like to end this book by presenting, not my own words but those of an old, respected, and impressive Cuban scholar—as a logical voice in counterpoint to the hostile views of critics in the U.S.A.

García Galló was for many years Professor of Classical Languages at the University of Santa Clara, and subsequently served as Chairman of the Department of Philosophy at the University of Havana. During those years he was a teacher of the future leader of the literacy struggle, Dr. Ferrer. Today in his seventies, Galló is a member of the Central Committee of the Communist Party. His special areas of concentration are in the realm of education and the sciences. In the course of a long conversation that we held in 1977, he spoke to me of the interlink between the pedagogic and political:

"When Fidel built the Liberation Army in the Sierra

Maestra, he endeavored to educate each soldier in his
forces who could not yet read or write. He educated, too,
the people of the local villages and farms—wherever he
might go. The rebel army would hold classes in the
mountains almost every night. The dual goal was always education *with* political analysis. The first was
never possible without the second.

"The so-called Culture of Silence, so much discussed
within the pedagogic circles of your nation, is in fact no
innocent or accidental matter. It does not happen just by
chance. It is the direct consequence of the oppression of
the poor. Their silence is broken first by revolution—
then by words."

He paused, then said: "I want to add one other point
as well. We in Cuba are thinking now in terms which
stand in direct contradiction to the U.S. point of view.
The U.S. sociologists mean, when they speak of 'the
power of speech,' only 'the word' itself. Yet mass participation in a human struggle is a form of speech as well.
Those who died in Chile speak forever with their blood.
Those who suffer in South Africa speak with their struggle. There are many different ways to break the silence,
but one step leads inevitably to the next. The process of
transformation does not need to occupy long genera-
tions. In our situation, we have been able to do a great
deal very, very fast . . .

"Therefore, we do not agree with this idea. Even
where there is a progressive government, it cannot mobilize the people as a revolutionary nation can. The poorest people still remain the ones who must be willing to
accept the least desirable work.

"In nations such as the United States the power
may appear, for various reasons, to be granted in
more generous helpings to the poor. It is never the
real thing. The power to *learn* may even seem to
have been granted to the poor; but it will never be

enough to let the poorest people know more than the way to operate machines—or, possibly, to read at the most shallow level, that which is least critical, least dangerous, and least profound . . ."

He paused again. "Well, of course, I mean these words in a symbolic sense. Obviously, there always are exceptions; but, by and large, the situation will be found, in every case, to be the same. In underdeveloped nations—Haiti, for example, where the rate of those who cannot read is in the eightieth percentile—here your government has no possible reason to develop even marginal skills such as those regarded as acceptable for the black and poor in the United States. Within these Third World nations U.S. corporations do not even *need* those kinds of workers who possess the middle-level competence afforded to such laborers in the U.S.

"It is difficult to say this to you, and I do not wish to hurt your feelings—as we have the faith that you have come here with an open mind and that you take an earnest point of view. But it is the truth that U.S. corporations almost always find their real self-interest in perpetuation of a partially illiterate and unskilled population."

Dr. Galló, much like many of the older educators whom I came to know in Cuba, frequently would soften the severity of his words by asking me about my personal life or telling a story at his own expense, often reminiscing on his struggles as a radical teacher under thirty years of terror from Machado to Batista. I found him a humane and cultivated man: elegant in his learning and reflective in appreciation of the literary classics that we spoke of for a time. He asked me whether I viewed myself primarily as a writer or "a man of politics."

I told him I knew that, by his ideology, he would not find it possible to separate the two ideas. I told him that this was, in general, my own opinion, too, but that I felt there ought to be a place for art and beauty also—literature and music in and of themselves.

"Everything," I said, "should not be relegated to a 'useful' role. Some things are worthy of our time and care only because they bring more beauty to the world."

To my surprise he did not disagree but urged me instead to try to get a ticket to a concert (an all-Mozart concert) that was being held that night. "It is very, very hard to get a ticket at this date. I have been told that it is almost totally sold out . . ."

Then, after pausing for another moment, he said this: "The Double Concerto of Bach is 'useful,' too, in my belief. If there were no Mozart, no Stravinsky, and no Bach and no Beethoven, all of our work, I think, would somehow be in vain. Who would desire to inherit the earth, only to find that trees no longer showered the streets with flowers in the spring—or that the Double Concerto, played by David Oistrakh and his son, had all at once been taken from the world?

"We would have won a revolution—for what goal? The stomach would be fed (and that would not be a small thing) but not the full potential of a human soul. The wretched of this earth *will* win their place beneath the sun someday; but, when they do, I like to think that there will still *remain* a sun up in the sky—and beautiful music flowing in the air."

At the door he spoke these final words: "Do you suppose that we are saying all of this so that you will write good things about our literacy struggle after you are back at home in the United States? It is a matter worth consideration . . .

"Go to the concert anyway—if you still can get a ticket! You can ask yourself the other question in the morning."

APPENDICES

RECORDS AND DOCUMENTS
OF THE LITERACY CAMPAIGN
Instructions for the Literacy Teacher

Fellow "alfabetizador":

Fill in the blanks clearly, preferably in print.

Do not hurry in answering the questions. The answers will come as a result of conversations with your pupil and of your observations while you work with him.

In the Observations section you are to write everything you consider of interest although not specified in the personal file.

You are to mark with an x on the time chart of the months and days of the year, the days you teach him. Leave blank the day you do not meet with him.

The number of x's will show the number of days worked.

In order to check the pupil's progress, three tests are given: Initial, Intermediate and Final.

Initial Test. Determines if the pupil is illiterate or semi-literate.

Illiterate. When the pupil is incapable of completing any of the exercises.

Semi-literate. When the pupil is able to complete the first three exercises or when he knows how to read but cannot write.

Intermediate Test. Verifies if the student is making progress, if he has difficulties and what are these difficulties. This test is given after the pupil finishes all of the exercises in lesson ≪Cuban Fishermen≫.

Final Test. Decides if the pupil knows how to read and write. It is given after the pupil has finished the primer ≪We Shall Conquer≫ and is able to read any easy material.

In addition, the pupil will write a letter to Dr. Fidel Castro, which will entitle him to receive a textbook to continue his studies.

These tests are not graded, because grading does not accurately measure the progress of the pupil. The ≪alfabetizador≫ is the only one who knows how the pupil is progressing and what are his difficulties.

Because of its revolutionary quality, our Campaign is clean and honest. Your work should equal it, ≪alfabetizador≫.

NATIONAL LITERACY COMMISSION

Municipal Commission of ....

QUESTIONNAIRE FOR ILLITERATES

No. ....

Date ....

I. NAME AND SURNAME:

....

Last   Middle   First

Sex: .... Age: ... Nationality: .... Marital Status: ......

II. RESIDENCE AND ZONE:

Street .... No. ....

between .... and ....

Barrio .... Farm ....

Municipality .... Province ....

Zone:

Urban: ☐

Rural: ☐   Sugar cane☐ Tobacco☐ Coffee☐ Livestock☐

Charcoal☐ Henequen☐ Mining☐ Others☐

III. OCCUPATION:

Present job ....

Place of work ....

Hours of work from .... to ....

IV. DATA FOR THE LITERACY CAMPAIGN

Have you ever attended school?   Yes☐   No☐

Do you know how to read?   Yes☐ No☐ A little☐

Do you know how to write?   Yes☐ No☐ A little☐

Why couldn't you learn before? ....

At what time do you study? ....

On what days of the week? ....

Observations: ....

V. DATA RELATIVE TO THE "ALFABETIZADOR" IN CHARGE OF THE QUESTIONNAIRE:

Name .... Telephone ....

Address: Street .... No. ...between ..... and ...

Municipality .... Province ....

Place where you teach reading and writing ....

```
┌─────────────────┐
│ No. . . . . . . . . . │
│─────────────────│
│ Date . . . . . . . . │
└─────────────────┘
```

NATIONAL LITERACY COMMISSION
Municipal Commission of . . . .
QUESTIONNAIRE FOR THE "ALFABETIZADOR"

NAME:

. . . .
     First   Middle   Last
Address . . . .
         Street   Number
Barrio . . . . Farm . . . .
Municipality . . . . Province . . . .

STUDIES COMPLETED:
In Primary School . . . .
Other studies . . . .
. . . .
. . . .
Occupation or profession . . . .
Works at . . . .
What hours could you devote to teaching? . . . .
Are you prepared to teach away from home? . . . .
INDICATE WHERE YOU COULD TEACH:
☐ In a classroom   ☐ At home
☐ In a center   ☐ At someone else's house
  (Cooperative, Union,   ☐ In another place
  School, etc.)
OBSERVATIONS: . . . .
. . . .
. . . .

. . . .
            Signature of "Alfabetizador"

NATIONAL LITERACY COMMISSION
THE PUPIL'S PERSONAL FILE

Complete name of pupil ....

....

Age .... Sex .... Marital status ....

Place of birth ....

....

Place of residence ....

Farm ....

Barrio........................ Municipality ....

Province .... Zone ....

Occupation ....

Date he (she) began to study ....

Date he (she) finished ....

Place where taught ....

Mark here the days you worked with your teacher:

(D A Y S)

MONTH	1	2	3	4	5	6	7	8	9	10	11	12	13	14	15	16	17	18	19	20	21	22	23	24	25	26	27	28	29	30	31
JANUARY																															
FEBRUARY ...																															
MARCH																															
APRIL........																															
MAY																															
JUNE																															
JULY																															
AUGUST																															
SEPTEMBER .																															
OCTOBER																															
NOVEMBER ..																															
DECEMBER ..																															

Total number of days worked ....

1. Why didn't he (she) learn how to read and write before? . . . .
    . . . .
    . . . .
2. Does he (she) attend classes regularly? . . . .
    . . . .
3. Is he (she) inclined to express his (her) ideas and opinions, or
    on the contrary, does he (she) talk little? . . . .
    . . . .
4. What does he (she) prefer?:
    Reading . . . .
    Writing . . . .
    Arithmetic . . . .
    Other preferences . . . .
5. Which points in the primer interest him (her) most? . . . .
    . . . .
6. What attitude does he (she) have toward studying?
    Interested? . . . .
    Indifferent? . . . .
    Reluctant? . . . .
7. Is he (she) happy in his (her) present work? . . . .
    . . . .
8. Does he (she) express a desire to improve himself (herself)
    through studying?
    . . . .
9. Observations . . . .
    . . . .
    . . . .
    . . . .

NATIONAL LITERACY COMMISSION
TECHNICAL DEPARTMENT
EVALUATION COMMISSION

Complete name of pupil ....
....
Address ....
Age........................ Sex ....
Date of test ....
Name of "alfabetizador" ....
Name of adviser ....

INITIAL TEST

1. Write your complete name ....
   ....
2. Write your address ....
   ....
3. Read:

loma	oso	piña
casa	dedo	fume

4. Dictation of these same words.
5. Read:

   > Toma un dedal.
   > Amo a Mimí.
   > El lee solo.

6. Dictation of the former.
7. Read:

   > Mañana iré a Viñales con los niños
   > Alquilé una cabañita. Veremos la cañada.

8. Dictation of the preceding paragraph.
9. Interpretation of the paragraph read.

NOTE: Numbers 4, 6 and 8 will be written on the reverse side of this page. On number 9, ask questions on what has been read.

NATIONAL LITERACY COMMISSION
TECHNICAL DEPARTMENT
EVALUATION COMMISSION

Complete name of pupil ....
....
Address ....
Age.......................... Sex ....
Date on which the test is taken ....
Name of "alfabetizador" ....
Name of adviser ....

INTERMEDIATE TEST

1. Write your complete name ....
   ....
2. Write your address ....
   ....
3. Read:

pesquería	cayo	arroyo
arado	avión	fusil
palma	comer	rocosa

4. Dictation of these same words.
5. Read:

   Mario limpia el arma.
   El sol sale por el este.
   El mar está quieto.
   Yara y Yumurí son ríos.

6. Dictation of the previous sentences.
7. Interpretation of the sentences read.

NOTE: Numbers 4 and 6 must be answered on the reverse side of the sheet. On number 7, ask questions about the sentences read. If the pupil is unable to read a word, return to the corresponding exercise in the primer to review it.

NATIONAL LITERACY COMMISSION
TECHNICAL DEPARTMENT
EVALUATION COMMISSION

Complete name of pupil ....

....

Address ....

Age.......................... Sex ....

Date of the test ....

Name of "alfabetizador" ....

Name of adviser ....

FINAL TEST

1. Write your complete name ....

....

2. Write your address ....

....

3. Read:

El Gobierno Revolucionario quiere convertir a Cuba en un país industrializado.

(The Revolutionary Government wants to convert Cuba into an industrialized country.)

Se crearán muchas industrias. Trabajarán muchos obreros. Se acabará el desempleo. (Many industries will be created. Many workers will have jobs. Unemployment will end.)

4. Answer the following questions:

What does the Revolutionary Government want? ....

What will be created? ....

What benefits will be obtained? ....

....

5. Dictation of the paragraph read.
6. Write Dr. Fidel Castro the letter he asked for.

NOTE: Question 5 should be answered on the reverse side of this page. The "alfabetizador" will send the letter addressed to Dr. Fidel Castro to the Municipal Council.

TEST RESULTS

INITIAL TEST
Date ....
Result: Illiterate ....Semi-literate ....
Verified by: ....Adviser
Observations: ....
....

INTERMEDIATE TEST
Date ....
Results: ....
....
Do you believe the results of this test correspond to the work of
the pupil in class? ....
....
Verified by ....Adviser
Observations: ....
....

FINAL TEST
Date ....
Results: ....
Learned how to read and write ... How long did he (she) take? .
Verified by ....Adviser
Observations: ....
....

....
Signature of the "Alfabetizador"

....
Signature of Teacher in Charge   Signature of the Adviser

HISTORICAL
TIMELINE

1853 July 28: José Martí, poet and "Apostle of the Cuban revolution," is born in Havana.

1868 October 10: The Ten Years War begins, the first major armed struggle for independence from Spain.

1895 May 19: José Martí is killed in battle against the Spanish on the plain of Boca de Dos Ríos.

1898 December 10: The Treaty of Paris grants Cuba independence.

1903 May 22: The signing of a permanent treaty between the U.S. and Cuba gives the U.S. control over Guantánamo naval base and full economic privileges in Cuba.

1925 August 16, 17: The Communist Party of Cuba is founded in Havana. Gerardo Machado, the manager of the American and Foreign Power and Light Company, is elected president of Cuba on a liberal ticket.

1926   August 13: Fidel Castro Ruz is born in Oriente Province, the son of a landowner.

1927   March 28: Machado forces a revision of the Cuban Constitution, granting himself a seven-year extension of his presidential term.

1930   April 19: Fifty thousand people demonstrate in Havana against the dictatorship of Machado.

1933   September 4: The "Sergeants' Revolt" and a general strike overthrow Machado. A military junta, headed by Fulgencio Batista, places in power Ramón Grau San Martín.

1934   January 15: Colonel Batista overthrows the government of Grau San Martín, placing Colonel Carlos Mendieta in the presidency as the first of three Batista governments.

1940   July 14: Fulgencio Batista is "elected" president of Cuba after ruling as *de facto* dictator since 1934.

1944   October 10: Grau San Martín replaces Batista as president.

1946   January: Fidel Castro is elected president of the Association of Law Students at the University of Havana.

1948   October 10: Carlos Prío Socarrás, Minister of Labor, is elected president.

1952   March 10: Fulgencio Batista executes a coup d'état, becomes dictator, abandoning the Constitution and dismissing the Congress.

1953   July 26: A force of one hundred and twenty young people, led by Fidel Castro, attack Fort Moncada in Santiago, Oriente Province. The attempt fails, but stirs dramatic response throughout the nation.

October 16: During his trial, Fidel Castro delivers his speech "History Will Absolve Me" and is sentenced to fifteen years in prison.

1954 In prison on the Isle of Pines, Fidel Castro begins organizing the Movement "of the Twenty-Sixth of July."

1955 May: Batista grants amnesty; Fidel Castro returns to Havana.
July: Fidel Castro flees to Mexico and begins to organize for armed invasion. He meets the Argentine physician Ernesto Che Guevara.

1956 November 25: The yacht *Granma* leaves Mexico with eighty-two men and women and arrives in Cuba on December 2.
December 18–25: Following the battle between the *Granma*'s army and Batista's troops at Alegría del Pío, the twelve survivors form the first Cuban guerrilla center in the Sierra Maestra.

1957 August: After months of repression and the police shooting of Frank País, a student leader of the urban resistance, Fidel Castro organizes a second rebel column led by Che Guevara in the Sierra Maestra.

1958 March 10: A Second Front is opened by Raúl Castro in northern Oriente.
August 29: Two columns, led by Che Guevara and by Camilo Cienfuegos, invade the provinces of Las Villas and Camagüey.
December 31: Santa Clara, capital of Las Villas Province, falls to the rebel forces. Batista flees to the Dominican Republic.

1959 January 2: Fidel Castro proclaims 1959 the "Year of Liberation" as the rebels capture Santiago.

January 8: Fidel Castro, preceded by Che and Camilo, enters Havana.

February 13: Fidel becomes prime minister.

July 18: Dr. Osvaldo Dorticós is appointed president of the republic.

November 26: Che is appointed director of the National Bank. U.S. investments in Cuba stand at approximately one billion dollars.

1960 August 6: The Cuban government nationalizes sugar mills, refineries, and the telephone company.

September 14: Dr. Castro leaves for New York City, where he addresses the U.N. and makes first reference to the Literacy Campaign.

October 19: The U.S. bans all exports to Cuba (except medicine and foodstuffs) as Fidel Castro nationalizes all remaining U.S. enterprises.

1961 January 3: The U.S. breaks off diplomatic relations with Cuba.

January 5: Conrado Benítez, a young black "alfabetizador," is assassinated by counter-revolutionaries in the Escambray.

April 1: The Literacy Campaign, in organizational stages for six months, begins in earnest. Student brigadistas soon arrive at Varadero Beach for training sessions.

April 15: An air raid on the Havana and Santiago airports kills seven people and wounds fifty-three. On April 17 expeditionary forces, financed and trained by the CIA in Guatemala, land at Playa Girón and Playa Larga ("the Bay of Pigs"). Within seventy-two hours twelve hundred invaders are captured and the invasion is declared a failure. On April 25 the U.S. declares a total embargo on trade with Cuba.

1962   The OAS (Organization of American States) excludes Cuba from the Inter-American system.
October 14–28: The U.S. discovers Soviet ballistic missiles in Cuba and asks Khrushchev to withdraw them. Khrushchev orders removal of the missiles.

1963   Fidel Castro travels to the Soviet Union for the first time.

1964   July: The OAS imposes a trade sanction upon Cuba, with only food and medicine exempted, and agrees to sever all diplomatic relations with the Cuban government.

1965   Castro states, "Major Ernesto Che Guevara will be found where he is most useful to the revolution." A newly constituted Cuban Communist Party is founded.

1967   October 8: Che Guevara is summarily executed in Bolivia after having attempted to organize a peasant revolt against the government. Agrarian reform, in its final stages, transfers all private land-holdings in Cuba to collective farms.

1968   March 13: Castro begins a major revolutionary offensive, nationalizing all trade, services, and private firms.

1970   June: The students of the first new junior high *en campo* ask Fidel to name it "School of the Martyrs of Kent" in memory of four students shot by the Ohio National Guard at Kent State University one month earlier.

1971   March: A new vagrancy law goes into effect. All unemployed people older than seventeen years are sent to re-education centers where they are given training in essential skills in order to be able to obtain useful employment. The guiding themes are "the discipline of work" and the importance of collective production.

1975 Cuba celebrates the First Congress of the Communist Party. Fidel congratulates the U.S. on report of the Senate Select Committee to Study Governmental Operations with Respect to Intelligence Activities. He calls the investigation a "positive step" for the U.S. in revealing CIA involvement in assassination attempts against him and other revolutionary leaders.

1977 June 13: Castro releases ten U.S. "political prisoners" and declares his willingness to free all prisoners if the U.S. will relinquish Guantánamo and lift the total trade embargo.

BIBLIOGRAPHY

BOOKS

(Alphabetical by author. Books without listed editors or authors, are cited alphabetically by title. Books published by the Cuban government are listed under separate heading.)

Alleged Assassination Plots Involving Foreign Leaders. Senate Select Committee to Study Governmental Operations with Respect to Intelligence Activities, Washington, November 20, 1975.

Barkin, David and Manitzas, Nita, eds., *In Cuba: The Logic of the Revolution.* Andover, Mass., Warner Publications, 1973.

Bhola, H.S., *Literacy Teachers for Adults.* Tanzania, UNESCO/UNDP, 1970.

Bonachea, Rolando and Valdez, Nelson, *Revolutionary Struggle, Selected Works of Fidel Castro, Vol. 1.* Cambridge, MIT Press, 1972.

Bronfenbrenner, Urie, *Two Worlds of Childhood: U.S. and U.S.S.R.* New York, Pocket Books, 1970.

Cardenal, Ernesto, *In Cuba.* New York, New Directions, 1974.

Dumont, René, *Is Cuba Socialist?* London, André Deutsch, 1970.

Ewer, Helen, Hageman, Alice, and Hedlund, Sonja, *Cuba: 100 Years of Struggle.* New York, Cuba Resource Center, 1970.

The Experimental World Literacy Programme: A Critical Assessment. Paris, UNESCO, 1976.

Fagen, Richard, *Cuba: The Political Content of Adult Education.* Stanford, Stanford University Press, 1964.

Fagen, Richard, *The Transformation of Political Culture in Cuba.* Stanford, Stanford University Press, 1969.

Fagen, Richard, O'Leary, Thomas and Brody, Richard, *Cubans in Exile: Disaffection and the Revolution.* Stanford, Stanford University Press, 1968..

Freire, Paulo, *Cultural Action for Freedom.* Cambridge, Harvard Educational Review Reprints, 1970.

Freire, Paulo, *Pedagogy of the Oppressed.* New York, Herder and Herder, 1972.

Gerassi, John, ed., *Venceremos! The Speeches and Writings of Ernesto Che Guevara.* New York, Simon and Schuster, 1968.

Gillette, Arthur, *Cuba's Educational Revolution.* London, Fabian Society, 1972.

Gillette, Arthur, *Youth and Literacy.* New York, Paris, UNESCO, 1972.

Goodman, Paul, *Growing Up Absurd.* New York, Vintage Books, 1970.

Green, Gil, *Revolution Cuban Style.* New York, International Publishers, 1970.

Harman, David, *Community Fundamental Education.* Lexington, Mass., D.C. Heath and Company, 1974.

Huberman, Leo and Sweezy, Paul, *Socialism in Cuba.* New York, Monthly Review Press, 1969.

Hughes, Langston, *I Wonder as I Wander.* New York, Holt, Rinehart, 1956.

Karabel, Jerome and Halsey, A.H., *Power and Ideology in Education.* New York, Oxford University Press, 1977.

Karol, K.S., *Guerrillas in Power, The Course of the Cuban Revolution.* New York, Hill and Wang, 1970.

Kenner, Martin and Petras, James, eds., *Fidel Castro Speaks.* New York, Grove Press, 1969.

Leiner, Marvin, *Children Are the Revolution: Day Care in Cuba.* New York, Viking Press, 1974.

Lewis, Oscar *et al.*, *Four Men: Living the Revolution, An Oral History of Contemporary Cuba.* Urbana, University of Illinois Press, 1977.

Lockwood, Lee, *Castro's Cuba, Cuba's Fidel.* New York, Random House, 1969.

Lorenzetto, Anna, *Lineamenti Storici e Teorici Dell'Educazione Permanente.* Rome, Vita Nova, 1976.

Lorenzetto, Anna and Neys, Karel, *Methods and Means Utilized in Cuba to Eliminate Illiteracy.* Havana, Cuban National Commission for UNESCO, 1965.

Mallin, Jay, ed., *Che Guevara on Revolution.* New York, Dell, 1969.

Matthews, Herbert, *Fidel Castro.* New York, Simon and Schuster, 1969.

Mesa-Lago, Carmelo, ed., *Revolutionary Change in Cuba.* Pittsburgh, University of Pittsburgh Press, 1971.

O'Connor, James, *Origins of Socialism in Cuba.* Ithaca, Cornell University Press, 1970.

Radosh, Ronald, ed., *The New Cuba.* New York, William Morrow, 1976.

Rius (Eduardo del Rio), *Cuba for Beginners.* New York, Pathfinder Press, 1970.

Ruiz, Ramon, *Cuba, Making of a Revolution.* New York, W.W. Norton, 1970.

Russell, Philip, *Cuba in Transition.* Austin, Armadillo Press, 1971.

Seers, Dudley, ed., *Cuba, Economic and Social Revolution.* Westport, Greenwood Press, 1964.

Sidel, Ruth, *Women and Child Care in China.* Baltimore, Penguin Books, 1972.

Sutherland, Elizabeth, *The Youngest Revolution.* New York, Dial Press, 1968.

Thomas, Hugh, *The Cuban Revolution.* New York, Harper and Row, 1971.

Tolstoi, Leo, *On Education.* Chicago, University of Chicago Press, 1968.

Yglesias, José, *In the Fist of the Revolution.* New York, Random House, 1968.

For further information on Cuba, contact:

The Cuba Resource Center. A church-supported organization, the CRC works to promote communication between people in Cuba and the United States and publishes *Cuba Review*. (Subscriptions to *Cuba Review*, a monthly publication, are five dollars per year.)

CONTACT: P.O. Box 206
             Cathedral Station
             New York, NY 10025

The Center for Cuban Studies, a resource center for films, books, and speakers.

CONTACT: 220 East 23rd Street
             New York, NY 10010

ARTICLES IN MAGAZINES
AND JOURNALS

(Alphabetical by author, unless citation is to entire issue.)

Araujo, Max Figueroa, "The Cuban School in the Countryside." *Prospects*, Vol. VI, No. 1, 1976.
Bengelsdorf, Carolee, "A Large School of Government." *Cuba Review*, Vol. VI, No. 3, September 1976.
Bowles, Samuel, "Cuban Education and the Revolutionary Ideology." *Harvard Educational Review*, Vol. 41, No. 4, November 1971.
"CIA: Conspiracy Makers." *Cuba Review*, Vol. VI, No. 2, June 1976.
Convergence. (Ontario Institute for Studies in Education), Vol. 1, No. 3, September 1968.
"Fidel 74." *Cuba Review*, Vol. IV, No. 3, 1974.
Freire, Paulo, "Literacy and the Possible Dream." *Prospects*, Vol. VI, No. 1, 1976.
Harman, David, "The Experimental World Literacy Program: A

Critical Assessment" (review.) *Harvard Educational Review*, Vol. 47, No. 3, August 1977.

Lorenzetto, Anna, "Una Rivoluzione Culturale." *I Problemi della Pedagogia*, May/June 1966.

Lorenzetto, Anna, "The Experimental Projects Sponsored by UNESCO and the Revolutionary Element in Literacy." *Convergence* (Ontario Institute for Studies in Education), Vol. 1, No. 3, September 1968.

"To be Educated is to be Free." *Cuba Review*, Vol. V, No. 2, June 1975.

Ward, Fred, "Cuba Today." *National Geographic*, January 1977.

Womack, John, Jr., "An American in Cuba." *New York Review of Books*, August 4, 1977.

PUBLICATIONS OF THE CUBAN GOVERNMENT

(Items alphabetical by title)

Alfabeticemos, manual para el alfabetizador. Havana, Ministry of Education, 1961.

Alfabetización: Nacionalización de la enseñanza. Havana, Ministry of Education, 1961.

Bohemia, Vol. 68, No. 52, December 24, 1976. See "La Campaña No Fue Un Milagro," Raúl Ferrer.

Cuba: Organización de la educación, 1973–1975. Havana, Ministry of Education, 1975.

Documentos directivos para el perfeccionamiento del subsistema de formación y perfeccionamiento del personal pedagógico. Havana, Ministry of Education, 1976.

Documentos directivos para el perfeccionamiento del subsistema de la educación de adultos. Havana, Ministry of Education, 1976.

Documentos directivos para el perfeccionamiento del subsistema de la educación técnica y profesional. Havana, Ministry of Education, 1976.

Documentos directivos para el perfeccionamiento del sistema nacional de educación. Havana, Ministry of Education, 1976.

Educación, Vol. VII, No. 24, 1977.

Educación, Vol. V, No. 19, October/December, 1975. See "Persepolis: Simposio de Alfabetización," Abel Prieto Morales.

Educación de adultos en Cuba, Raúl Ferrer. Havana, Ministry of Education, 1976.

Education in Revolution (English, Spanish and French editions). Havana, Cuban Institute of Books, 1975.

La educación en Cuba. Havana, Ministry of Education, 1973.

Lectura campesina. Havana, Ministry of Education, 1973.

Libro del sexto grado, Vademecum, Raúl Ferrer et al. Havana, Ministry of Education, 1977.

Manual de educación formal. Havana, Ministry of Education, 1976.

Martí: Anti-Imperialist, Emilio Riog de Leuchsenring. Havana, Book Institute, 1967.

Martí en los Estados Unidos (Obras Completas, Vol. 13.) Havana, Editorial Nacional, 1964.

Orientaciones para el Brigadista. Havana, Ministry of Education, 1961.

Venceremos. Havana, Ministry of Education, 1961.

NOTES

(See Selected Bibliography for further data on all books listed in these notes.)

p. xiv   Quotation from Fidel Castro on turning fortresses into schools is taken from a speech delivered November 27, 1959. The source is *Educação em Revolução*, Iniciativas Editoriais, Lisbon, 1976, pp. 13–15. The English translation is that of Dr. Freire.

               Quotation from Fidel Castro on the true teacher, drawn from a speech delivered July 18, 1966, is found on p. 48 of the text cited above.

p. 4   My own quotations from Dr. Castro are drawn primarily from two English-language sources: *Fidel Castro Speaks* (Martin Kenner and James Petras), *The Transformation of Political Culture in Cuba* (Richard Fagen). With the help of Martha Acosta I have at times attempted to render certain passages more faithful by substitution of idiomatic for literal translations.

233

For the full text, in translation, of Fidel's four-and-a-half-hour speech to the General Assembly of the United Nations on September 26, 1960, see Kenner and Petras, pp. 3–36.

p. 5   Source of initial illiteracy figures: UNESCO Report of 1965, *Methods and Means Utilized in Cuba to Eliminate Illiteracy*, p. 15.

p. 6   For exact statistics on the ages, numbers, origins, and educational levels of the student volunteers, see *Methods and Means*, pp. 16, 27, 45; Fagen, pp. 45–47; "The Literacy Campaign and Adult Education," by Richard Jolly, in *Cuba, The Economic and Social Revolution*, ed. by Dudley Seers, pp. 195, 197, 200–202.

p. 7   See *Lucia, Part III* and *The New School* (Cuban Institute of Film) for graphic examples of the motivation process, both for learners and for teachers. These films are distributed by Tricontinental Film Center, 333 Sixth Avenue, New York, N.Y. 10014.

p. 9   Fagen describes the Coca-Cola ad in these words: "With what was undoubtedly unintended irony, an advertisement for the soon-to-disappear Coca-Cola company showed the lily-white and well-manicured hand of the lady of the household (with a Coke bottle nearby) guiding the darker and rougher hand of a domestic servant through the ABC's" (p. 57). The version of this story (as well as samples of the posters that were used to mobilize the young), described or shown to me in Cuba, differ a bit from Fagen's versions, but highlight most of the same points.

p. 11   "The Attendance Plan," created to provide activities for children while the schools were closed, is described in Fagen, p. 51, as well as in *Methods and Means*, p. 39.

p. 12   U.S. poet Langston Hughes emphasizes the point that the Cuban color line was relatively flexible until the arrival of those U.S. citizens who established the first of Cuba's resort hotels, bringing their quota of racial prejudice from the mainland: "Hotels that formerly were lax in their application of the color line, now discourage even Mulatto Cubans, thus seeking the approval of their American clientele." See Langston Hughes, *I Wonder as I Wander*, pp. 10–15.

p. 12 ff   A few copies of the primer and the manual still exist. So far as I know, they are unavailable outside of Cuba.

p. 15   Quotations from *Orientaeiones para el Brigadista:* see pp. 2 and 3.

p. 18   Freire's methods and practice in Brazil are described in detail in *Cultural Action for Freedom* (an autobiographical discussion of his literacy work) as well as in his later works.

p. 21   Further details on the Varadero training camp are provided by Fagen, pp. 43–44. I have relied upon Fagen's scholarly work to corroborate and sometimes rectify a number of details, mainly descriptive, that I first had drawn from tapes and notes.

p. 22   Ruth Sidel makes this statement in regard to China in the years following the Chinese Revolution: "The Chinese were also faced with the traditional divorce between physical and intellectual labor which Isaac Deutscher characterizes as the 'divorce that has been at the root of man's estrangement from man, of mankind's division into rulers and ruled and into antagonistic classes . . .' " *Women and Child Care in China*, p. 72. Mier Febles is quoted on the reconciliation of the city and the country: interview with the author in Havana, September 1976.

p. 25   For these and later excerpts from Fidel's address, I have relied, with minor idiomatic alterations, upon the translation offered by Fagen, pp. 180–192.

Abel Prieto's booklet on courtesy as "revolutionary style" is a publication intended for classroom use: *Manual de educación formal*, issued by the Cuban Ministry of Education.

p. 29   The stated teacher-pupil ratio of one-to-two was itself a come-down from Fidel's initial goal: "To every illiterate, a teacher; to every teacher, a pupil." The government's adaptation of initial goals to ultimate realities is summarized in *Methods and Means*, p. 43.

p. 29   For further breakdown figures on the ratio of students to teachers, see Jolly in Seers, ed., pp. 194–195.

p. 31   Oriente was one of the six provinces of Cuba at the time of my first visit. Beginning in 1977, however, the nation was divided into fourteen newly designated provinces. Oriente itself was divided into five.

p. 45   Freire is quoted from *The Pedagogy of the Oppressed*, p. 31.

p. 46   The figure of 21,000 is itself disputed in the UNESCO text, with the impression given, in at least one passage, that a realistic figure for the "worker volunteers" as a consequence of attrition (or of inaccurate figures at the start) was more like 13,000. Whichever number we accept, the figures appear to represent a clear-cut disappointment from the point of view of those in Cuba who had been accustomed to unqualified and exuberant responses to a government appeal. According to Ferrer, the figures are not so disturbing as they first appear. Thousands of workers, although they did not leave their homes, nonetheless increased the numbers of the "People's Teachers." (Interview with author, September 1976).

p. 47   According to Ferrer, there were 45,000 certified teachers in Cuba at the time Batista fell. Approximately 10,000 had no class-assignments. If this figure is relied upon (a figure Jolly uses too) then the apparent goal of the September "teachers' draft" was to bring into the literacy struggle those 10,000 "missing teachers" who had not been part of the first wave of 35,000 volunteers. (The remaining 10,000 were not, of course, identical with those 10,000 teachers who did not have jobs. Indeed, many of those teachers who had been without jobs prior to the revolution proved, as a consequence, to be more sympathetic to the revolution and were frequently the first to answer the government appeals.)

p. 47   The residual conflicts in Cuba's post-revolutionary Left are discussed by Fagen, pp. 104–106.

pp. 50–51   In spite of similar efforts in the sugar harvest of 1970 ("The Ten Million Tons"), the advertised goal was never reached. In our interview, however, Prieto observed that, despite this disappointment, the 1970 harvest was nearly double that of any year before the revolution. Prieto also insists that the sugar harvest and the literacy struggle were treated with equal enthusiasm by the people. The striking success of the latter, he believes, was an example of the triumph of "unfettered human effort" after many years of exploitation. The harvest, on the other hand, was plagued by technological and technical dilemmas, lack of adequate equipment, and the like. None of these factors would have been of more than marginal importance in the literacy struggle.

pp. 52   The first of these two letters to Fidel is found in *Socialism in Cuba*, by Huberman and Sweezy, p. 25. The second was copied from the archives of the Literacy Museum during my visit of 1976.

p. 54   See Jolly p. 204, and the excellent summary in Chapter Three of Fagen for most of these statistics. Dr. Ferrer provided the most recent government figures in our interview of 1976. The 1953 census figures are found in *Educación de adultos en Cuba*, Raúl Ferrer, p. 12. The Latin American median for functional illiteracy (32.5 percent) is found in Huberman and Sweezy, p. 28. UNESCO's estimate for the U.S. is found in *The UNESCO Statistical Yearbook*, 1973. Estimate given by *The New York Times* is cited and discussed in *Illiteracy In the United States* (David Harman and Carman Hunter), a private publication of the Ford Foundation, April 20, 1978. (See p. i of preface.) Estimates for initial reduction in Cuban illiteracy rate are my own.

pp. 55–56   For further statistics on the Follow-Up, see Jolly, pp. 211–214.

p. 57   My conversation with David Harman took place in November 1976 at his home in Cambridge.

Figures for active workers now enrolled in Cuban universities are based on my conversation with Minister of Education Fernández, in September, 1976. According to Fernández, there were 120,000 enrollments in 1976 with 5,000 additional students attending foreign universities. It seems realistic to expect the total university enrollment to pass 150,000 by 1980.

p. 58   Fidel's speech of December 22, 1961 was recounted to me in the course of conversation with Dr. Ferrer.

p. 66   Teacher-pupil ratio today in Cuban schools appears to average one-to-twenty-five—with a second teacher almost always doing practice teaching in the same room.

The Family Code, a major step in equalizing rights of women, went into effect in 1975.

pp. 72, 73   For UNESCO's official report on the worldwide literacy program, see *The Experimental World Literacy Programme: A Critical Assessment* (UNESCO); for an unofficial and more informative report, see *Community Fundamental Education* by David Harman, pp. 47–70, as well as H.S. Bhola's *Literacy Teachers of Adults*, pp. 11–12.

John Simmons' purported findings in Madagascar and Algeria were recounted to me in my interview with David Harman.

p. 74   Author's memo based on telephone interview with Schwana Tropp, December 14, 1976.

p. 75   Dr. Lorenzetto's findings are published in an article entitled "The Experimental Projects Sponsored by UNESCO and the Revolutionary Element in Literacy," *Convergence*, September, 1968, pp. 31–36.

pp. 77–78   In a letter written in reply to my inquiry Dr. Lorenzetto emphasized her wish to "confirm all that I wrote in my report," and went on to inform me of some matters that neither I nor Cuban leaders yet had known: "In this

connection, since you have asked whether I have something else to add, I would indeed like to say that UNESCO,
upon sending my report on the Literacy Campaign to
Cuba, cut out one third of my original paper." This, she
said, one could "easily verify by reading the original
integral Italian edition . . . published in 1966 in the
Review edited by the University of Rome." She added
these remarks: "I never did say anything about this
matter to my Cuban friends, in order not to exacerbate
their bitterness towards UNESCO. But I think the moment has now come to tell the truth, and I am glad you
did encourage me to do so."

p. 78   Source for this exchange, denied or else forgotten by
UNESCO personnel, is my interview with Dr. Ferrer,
since confirmed in subsequent conversation.

pp. 78–79   In his letter of May 4, 1977, Mr. Fobes explains the
unavailability of the UNESCO report on Cuba. "At this
writing, I cannot tell you how many copies were printed
by the Cubans, how many they distributed or how, nor
cite the several published references to the report on the
Cuban experience. It was not concealed." He goes on to
say, "The Cuban success does not shame UNESCO; it
may make some governments wish that they had been
able to emulate it—that all the factors (including courage) had been present in their particular situations to
permit a similar experience . . ."

pp. 80–81   For quotations from Dr. Lorenzetto, see *Convergence*,
cited above, p. 32, and *Methods and Means*, pp. 72–73.

p. 82   Cuba's continuing efforts in adult education are discussed by Arthur Gillette in *Youth and Literacy*, published by UNESCO. See pp. 53–55.

p. 88   My own impression confirms Prieto's claim, but it seems
important to remind the reader that I was in Cuba (1976)
only for six weeks, then again (1977) for even fewer
weeks. Elizabeth Sutherland, who was living in Cuba
during 1968, assesses the racial situation in interesting
detail in *The Youngest Revolution*, pp. 138–168.

p. 89 Dr. Castro's words, spoken at the beginning of 1959, were as follows: "They married us to the lie and they obliged us to live with it; for that reason it seems that the world collapses when we listen to the truth." The precise quotation, which Dr. Ferrer repeated by memory in our interview, is cited by Minister Fernández in a letter to me, dated November 24, 1977.

p. 89 At some point before these words were spoken by Fidel Castro, a similar statement had been voiced by Che Guevara: ". . . In moments of extreme danger it is easy to activate moral incentives; to maintain their effectiveness, it is necessary to develop a consciousness in which values acquire new categories. Society as a whole must become a huge school." The statement is from "Socialism and Man in Cuba," a letter to Carlos Quijano, editor of the Montevideo weekly *Marcha*. (Che's letter may be found in *Che Guevara on Revolution*, ed. by Jay Mallin, pp. 132–133.)

p. 92 The book of poems and stories for adults working at the elementary level, and containing Ferrer's poem "The Water," is entitled *Lectura campesina*. See pp. 83–85.

p. 108 The book to which Rosario García made "contributions" is a collection of short stories and political essays for adults at the lower-secondary level. It is one of many books of this sort published by the Cuban Ministry of Education.

p. 110 For documentation of CIA involvement in destruction of crops, poisoning of animals, and several planned assassinations of Fidel, see: *Alleged Assassination Plots Involving Foreign Leaders*, a report of the Senate Select Committee to Study Governmental Operations with Respect to Intelligence Activities, pp. 4–6, 71–180; CBS Reports, "The C.I.A.'s Secret Army," broadcast June 10, 1977; *The New York Times*, October 20–22, 1976, November 2, 1976; *The Washington Post*, January 9 and 17, 1977, October 16–21, 1976, March 21, 1977; *The Washington Star*, October 16 and 21, 1976; The New York *Daily News*, April 20–23, 1975; *Newsweek*, December 12, 1977; *Los Angeles Times,* January 27, 1977; *Boston Sunday Globe,* January 9, 1977 and March 6, 1977.

p. 110–111 Guevara on the right to higher education for those who fought at Playa Girón: *Venceremos! The Speeches and Writings of Che Guevara,* ed. by John Gerassi, p. 211.

p. 115 For further discussion of economic motivation in the education of adults, see Ferrer, cited above, p. 25.

p. 125 Martí's words are taken from a letter to the editor of *The Nation,* dated April 9, 1883, found in *Martí en los Estados Unidos,* p.53. The English used here is a free translation of Martí's passage, as rendered by Raúl Ferrer in conversation.

pp. 126–127 The present Development Plan, defining the overall program of required academic studies, went into effect in April, 1975. In 1980 an updated plan will go into effect. The requirements of the updated plan are detailed in *Documentos directivos para el perfeccionamiento del sistema nacional de educación,* pp. 20–21, 25–26.

p. 132 Jolly gives statistics for prerevolutionary school attendance in Seers, ed., pp. 220–224.

p. 136 A year later, Fernández stated, in our second interview, that this might prove to be an overly high estimate. By late 1977 there were above 500 "lower-level secondary" schools *en campo.* Construction-plans for 85 additional schools each year promise a total of 750 schools by 1980. Without a sudden economic spurt (and consequent increase in construction-plans), the figure of one thousand schools for half-a-million kids by 1980 cannot plausibly be reached. The goal of reaching the one-thousand mark by 1985 seems more realistic.

p. 158 Quotations from *Practical English* are reconstructed here from notes and tape. Copies of the book are available from the Cuban Ministry of Education.

p. 160 On the issue of capital punishment there is no room for argument, at least as far as whether it exists or not. It *does.* A policy described by Carlos as "a great mistake" is the present-day reality in Cuba. As in the U.S. and the U.S.S.R., capital punishment is openly conceded by the government to be the last resort in certain areas of crime regarded as most dangerous. In the Cuban situation this includes the violation of minors, murder, treason, criminal assault on essential social property (e.g., destruction of the food supply), and armed robbery of an inhabited house. In the above-cited letter to this author from Minister Fernández, the minister writes: "One must point out that these cases are very few. Years pass without applying it [i.e., capital punishment]."

On the question of imprisonment for one's beliefs, there is, of course, a vast amount of international criticism of Cuba—but much uncertainty as to the facts themselves. According to Cuban sources, there are less than twenty prisoners of U.S. citizenship in Cuba, the first of whom were arrested in 1959, with most recent arrests in 1966. The Cubans insist that these Americans were legally convicted of crimes, allegedly CIA activities, against the Cuban government. Fidel has opened discussion on these prisoners with the U.S. State Department. When challenged on the issue of human rights, however, he is adamant that Cuba will learn nothing of human rights and justice from a government that has attempted his own assassination fourteen times and which consistently supports the most brutal totalitarian regimes of Latin America and Asia. (Information on this issue is found in The *Boston Sunday Globe,* March 6, 1977, *Boston Globe,* August 11, 1977, and *The New York Times,* August 12, 1977.)

p. 186   For further details on the Martí School, see *Granma Weekly Review,* English edition, September 11, 1977.

p. 187   This material is drawn from on-site interview. Most of the data are confirmed by Carnoy and Werthein in an excellent study, "Socialist Ideology and the Transformation of Cuban Education," in *Power and Ideol-*

ogy in Education (Jerome Karabel and A. H. Halsey), p. 587.

p. 190   The French author René Dumont, viewed with cautious interest by certain segments of North American opinion but designated without qualification by Cuban leaders as a paid agent of the CIA, has written a sarcastic, at times vindictive, work in which he strongly criticizes Fidel Castro for his active participation in such specifics as crossbreeding, animal genetics, and the like. For Dumont's views, see *Is Cuba Socialist?*, pp. 106, 107.

p. 196   Needless to say, I do not have in mind as an approach that I admire the use of the story of "Mr. Sawyer" and his wife. I have made reference to that book because I do not like to bypass an archaic throwback if, by some misfortune, it is still in active use. Most of the Cuban texts that I have seen do not appear to constitute the Marxist parallels to those old and soul-destroying "readers" which for so many years have been our teachers' bane and children's curse.

POSTSCRIPT

John Womack, in discussion of a recent book on Cuba (*New York Review of Books*, August 4, 1977), made the observation: "A contemporary book about a revolution has to be an aftervision . . . Revolutionary changes happen so fast and so unpredictably . . . The Cubans, in particular, have defied prediction." He is, of course, correct. I have attempted, for this reason, not only to keep pace with all the latest changes prior to the day my writing goes to press, but also to leave open, as unanswered questions, almost every subject-area in which the goals are set but have not yet been reached. The risks and liabilities remain.

TO THE READER

Out of respect for the privacy or shyness of several people, both children and adults, I have used pseudonyms for various non-public persons portrayed within this book. I have also, on occasion, condensed two interviews or spliced two conversations in order to avoid unnecessary repetition of arrivals and departures, of endings and beginnings. At no point, however, is dialogue used within this book which was not spoken by a public administrator, friend, pupil or teacher in the Cuban schools. All public figures, of course, as well as Pedro Sánchez, Martha Acosta, Armando Valdez, and the principals of every school described, are identified—if identified at all—by their real names.

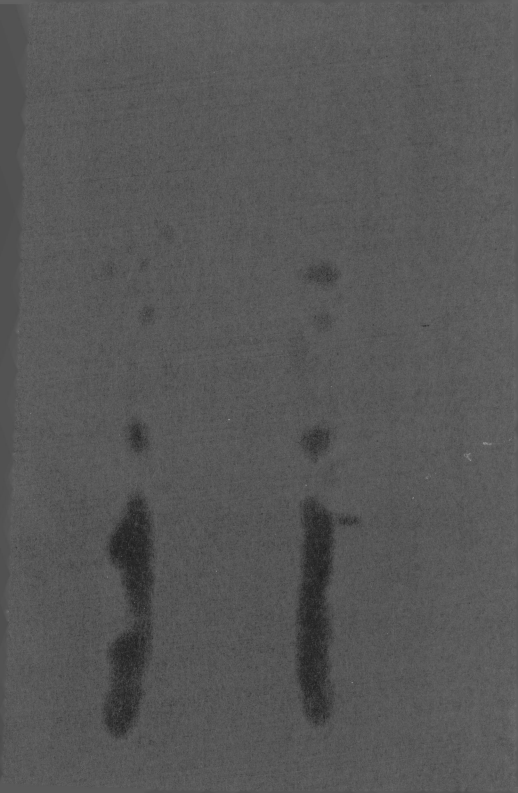

DATE DUE

GAYLORD

PRINTED IN U.S.A.